ISSUES IN THE WAKE OF VATICAN II

Proceedings of the Eighth Convention of the Fellowship of Catholic Scholars

March 22 - 24, 1985
Chicago, Illinois

Chairman and President

Rev. Earl A. Weis, S.J.
Loyola University of Chicago

Proceedings of the Eighth Convention
of the Fellowship of Catholic
Scholars

ISSUES IN THE WAKE
OF VATICAN II

edited by
Paul L. Williams

Northeast Books

A division of the Cultural Society of Northeastern Pennsylvania,
a non-profit corporation
Scranton, Pennsylvania

ISSUES IN THE WAKE OF VATICAN II

Published with ecclesiastical approval

ISBN 0—937374—02—4

Cover Design by Saks & Pilling

Associate Editor: Gerard E. Grealish

Typeset by Ron Semian at Design Print, Inc.

Layout by Kim Schemerhorn

Northeast Books Edition 1985
by special arrangement with the
Fellowship of Catholic Scholars

TABLE OF CONTENTS

Magnetic Fields of Theology:
An Historical Estimation

by

Msgr. Eugene V. Clark

The magnetic fields to which I refer are those endemic pressures that distract, even tear Catholic scholars from their proper work. Hardly an age has failed to produce them. These pressures are created by a wide range of passions — high ones like love of the truth and the imitation of Christ; and fearful ones like love of place and power, venality, and hatred of one's opponents. All these and other powerful human currents have swept honest scholars — not to mention others — far from the harbors of unfettered research and disinterested reflection. Indeed, it is my thesis that most often, and especially when major issues rise within the Catholic community, it is extremely difficult for scholars not to be imperiously co-opted by the partisans.

Surely some scholars voluntarily abandon the high ground and rejoice in a match with any street fighter. They are not the center of our interest this evening. We are interested in the fields themselves as destructive pressures on those who love the truth; and how difficult these pressures make it for scholars to shake off the passions of any age.

More often than not in Christian history it was extremely difficult for scholars to stay free of such magnetic pulls, and, in many generations, only scholars of high vision and motivation rose above the importunings of honest partisans. Even more subtly, scholars sometimes succumbed to an estimable personal desire to solve the painful problems of the age. But, in so far as they were problem-solvers, volunteers or not, they made it difficult for themselves to think and write with the detachment and freedom required for lovers of final truth.

Positively, we may put it this way. Since intellectual strife and partisan exchange among Christians never fade, since it is extremely difficult for interested persons not to enter into such conflicts, since great values are often the subject of such strife and the possible loss of such values alarms good men and women, and since the development of Christian doctrine has taken place in no small measure, through the abrasions of such conflicts, we conclude that many fine scholars either (a) have been drawn into service in the conflicts and been lost in the search for objective Christian truth, or (b) have been so distracted by the furies of conflict that they have lost their focus, or (c) have been so abused by partisans that they have lost heart.

What can we conclude from this? Namely, that it takes something more than a fine mind and good intentions to serve the cause of truth and to make a positive contribution to the sound and universal development of Christian doctrine. It requires considerable courage and strength of character to suffer the taunts of those who consider a response to the spirit of the age a spiritual imperative, and who accuse those who respond to a higher love of truth of being contemptuous of the age and its human problems. This is a bitter charge and only men and women of virtue can bear it. Intellect is not safe without virtue, as Newman never ceased to tell us.

And what rare balance of mind it takes to assist those who seek the truth in the flawed language of any age, and to respond to it without patronizing or succumbing to it.

Let us consider three cases among many that are available to us.

The Miletians

Only a generation after Saint Paul there appeared among Christians a tendency to consider the Church as a body of saints. Absolute sinlessness, such Christians theorized, was required of the baptized since there could be no second Baptism. The sentiment was made explicit by the Encratists who said that Baptism demanded celibacy, that marriage was an evil, and that there was little hope for the reconciliation of sinners.

But everyday living and common sense challenged this. Moreover, an unresolvable extreme encouraged radical solutions in the opposite direction. The durable Gnostics upheld such an antithesis, saying that since sin comes from matter it cannot affect the spirit and is, therefore, of small importance in any circumstance.

The surviving literature of the time suggests that the rigorist Encratist opinion was widespread, albeit always a minority view. It convinced many that post-baptismal sin was most difficult to forgive. We understand this sentiment best if we see it against the background of a pagan world, a world of exhibitionist licentiousness in which these Christians lived.

A more reasonable view appeared in the **Shepherd** by Hermas, a Roman priest. He saw God's pardon always available to repentant sinners. But he also saw the repentant sinner re-entering active communion in the Church only after substantial acts of penance.

Tertullian (160-220), in his early days an extraordinary benefactor of theology in the West, followed the emerging Roman view that God's direct forgiveness was always available to repentant sinners, but developed the concept of a ritual called *Exomologesis* — the well known laborious public penance by which a sinner atoned for his sin, a penance the Church made efficacious for re-entry into full communion. Persons guilty of apostasy, murder or fornication could not re-enter communion through *Exomologesis.* No one seemed clear how such persons might return to communion. Common opinion assumed they were barred for life.

The practice of *Exomologesis* lasted barely more than a generation since only the unreservedly pious accepted the practice. Less resolute penitents dodged it. Secret sinners abounded. In the face of this, others began deferring Baptism. The system was soon seen as counterproductive.

But a theological point had been made by Tertullian — namely, that there was probably no forum for re-entry into communion for apostates. It was not unchallenged, but the theory now had a reputable provenance.

A generation and a bit later, the persecution of Decian (249-251) and subsequent persecutions put the sin of apostasy into a new context. These persecutions were far better organized and systematic than prior ones which had touched small percentages of Christians. Now, almost every known Christian was challenged by the authorities who were less determined to kill them than to bring them back into line. A variety of perfunctory compromises were permitted by the authorities, who were combatting defiance more than religious dissent. Confiscation of all property was the normal penalty for a defiant Christian; but magistrates freely gave out "certificates of sacrifice" to anyone who would take one, without requiring any active pagan worship. Martyrs were relatively few: imprisoned, loyal confessors were numerous. They suffered abuse and fiscal ruin. The number of technical apostates who took certificates was very large.

Now the problem of readmission was posed as a truly momentous problem.

There was an interesting side door for readmission to public communion in the Church. Readmission had been granted by many Bishops to *lapsi* who won the intercession of an imprisoned confessor.

The intercession was to the Bishop for the *lapsi's* readmission. This was a happy solution for a while. Then some confessors, perhaps worn down by importunings, granted wholesale intercessions. Mobs of *lapsi* sought such help from imprisoned confessors. One confessor granted intercession for all the *lapsi* of the world. Some Bishops, like Cyprian of Carthage, considered this wholesale process ridiculous. In 250, Cyprian decreed that he would consider intercessions only if given for individuals known to the confessor.

So while most apostates found oblique ways back into communion, the serious point had been raised that apostasy put a Christian in an especially difficult position and also that permission from the Church to re-enter liturgical and social communion after apostasy was more difficult to secure than God's personal forgiveness. *Lapsi* were not thought damned, and that they were not proved rather demoralizing for other Christians and created a serious problem of scandal.

Two other factors influenced Christian thinking: the desire of the Catholic community to make fortitude and loyalty normative standards among Christians; and, conversely, the desire to manifest its disapproval of the cynicism of many of the *lapsi*. After all, how did a Christian honor the martyrs with true piety, many of them friends and relatives, and also sit at table easily with *lapsi*? It was a problem not of meanness or thinking *lapsi* damned, but a matter of setting standards and avoiding the scandal that threatened to undermine them.

It was into this theological debate and social situation that Miletus (Bishop of Lycopolis in Upper Egypt) and his followers entered and drew the African Church into a theological war, creating a disruption of Church jurisdictions, schism, bloodshed, and general upheaval in the Christian community.

Miletus, not alone, rejoiced in strong positions. He leapfrogged over the earlier rigorists and declared that the compromisers, the *lapsi,* were not only separated from Church communion, but had lost the effects of Baptism. They required a re-baptism. Priestly and episcopal Orders and the ecclesiastical positions based on them were similarly vitiated by the delinquents' failure in fortitude.

Reasoning backward, the Miletians said that the common cause of personal failure in the face of martyrdom and the annulled Baptism was a prior defective conversion to Christ. Therefore, before re-baptism the Miletians agreed that a discernible severe penance was required as proof of a change of heart. A body of theology was created to support this position.

Opposition centered on the impossibility of re-baptism.

But the Miletian dissent was not born of theory or theology. Early in the development of Miletian views, Alexander, the Bishop of Alexandria, received back into communion a compromised Bishop without re-ordination or re-baptism and without the Tertullian sort of penance Miletus deemed necessary as a sign of reconversion. Miletus and his followers refused to recognize the bishop so received. Logically, they refused to recognize all bishops and priests who had been compromised. In the heat of argument, the Miletians declared that compromisers should not and perhaps could not be received back under any circumstances. In a matter of months, the Alexandrine Province became spotted with duplicate bishops, pastors, and deacons, all claiming that theology forbad them to recognize their opponents. Popular divisions reached the smallest villages, and violence often placed nominees in possession of pastorates.

While theology was the language of dispute, hardly anyone would have denied, nor can we, that the powerful source of Miletian demands was an underlying assumption that Christians who had withstood the imminent threat of martyrdom should not be governed, guided, preached at, and absolved by men who had not stood firm. Such relationships were not only unbecoming, they were downright annoying, humanly speaking. Popular sentiment was never really divided over theology. Miletians and their sympathizers thought of themselves not as theologians, but as loyal "friends of the martyrs." They thought honoring their heroic dead required a stern position regarding the *lapsi*. They thought of the *lapsi* the way a Gold Star Mother in 1945 might have thought of army deserters.

Theology, prior to Miletus' objections, had no basis on which to consider "re-baptism." While the idea of re-baptism had some academic credibility, it had little intellectual credibility. But it had tremendous credibility as a powerful popular sentiment that said compromisers in pastoral positions sharply lessened the militant spirit required of the Church and were demoralizing and unreliable in the face of future persecutions. Moreover, the *lapsi* violated the modesty expected of a sinner.

In a perfect world, the *lapsi* might have sensed the impolitic consequences of their return to pastoral office. But they did not. Nor could they retire from pastorates on the principle that re-baptism and re-ordination were required of them. That would betray their loyalty to both jurisdictional order and sound theology.

Despite the dilute theological roots of Miletianism, theologians were rapidly pressed into service. Who can say whether theologians plunged willingly into this conflict, or were required by the passions of the time to strengthen one side or the other? Until Miletus, the opponents of the *lapsi* lacked theological and ecclesiastical leverage. Miletus supplied a theology. However sincere the Miletian theologians may have been and however much they called for aid for their pro-martyr party, they did, indeed, become the intellectual sustainers of a deeply committed activist party which supported replacement bishops, deacons, and pastors.

Let us assume, as a fiction, that everyone involved in this dispute was utterly sincere; that the search for theological support was also honest and true; that theologians became sincere partisans of their causes. It is the situation of such honest men, hard-pressed by equally honest activists and the community pressures of the day, that produces the magnetic fields which, as I have suggested, have often carried off into violence whole Christian communities and also carried many theologians away from the true work of pursuing universal truth. Perhaps there wasn't a bad fellow in the whole lot of partisans — mean feeling and violence aside — but the origins, fuel, goals, and the methods were, almost every one of them, non-theological and basically corruptive of theology. Part of that corruption was that theologians were enlisted as partisans, not as advisors; another part was that the assumptions and final proofs on each side were put forward as if theology were the cause and norm of the debate. Theological process for a generation in North Africa served, at best, a popular ascetical sentiment; at worst, the violent pursuit of power. Theologians in this dispute were hardly allowed to serve the causes of theology.

Nor can the dialectic be invoked. The intervention of the Emperor and his magistrates to end the violence was hardly an intellectual resolution. Profitably, theologians were left with vitiated propositions and some new parameters. But few theologians had a chance to pursue the truth without severe distraction and pressure.

Of course, the Christian community gained some wisdom from the partisan struggles. The Church had learned one shocking lesson: that theology can be used for many goals other than the pursuit of truth.

Arianism

Our second case followed hard on the divisions of Miletianism. It was the riveting case of Arianism, an action in which some scholars see at work most of the hazards that will ever assail the Church. In Africa and in the East, it threatened a hierarchy already unnerved by irreconciled differences about the *lapsi* and the violence that accompanied them. Schism was in the air. Passion justified itself as a love of pure religion.

Arius, a priest of Alexandria, had been banned from his ministry as a Miletian. In a gesture of reconciliation when the issue seemed settled by authority, Bishop Alexander of Alexandria received Arius back and appointed him to a major Church.

I will not describe Arianism. But when Arius preached that Christ was not really God, Bishop Alexander, a fair and cultivated man, suggested a public debate. In it, Arius was manifestly worsted, and the provincial bishops disapproved Arius' views in a 98-to-2 vote.

Arius excelled in rhetoric, a discipline for persuasion. His priorities were not in theology: they were in party spirit and organization. He had tried confrontation as a Miletian and in preaching his theories on Christ's divinity, and he lost publicly in each case.

Arius was the quintessential party man. He expected friends never to forget him. Licking his wounds, he wrote to friends and old schoolmates. Among them his persuasive powers were not shadowed by his public losses in Alexandria. He wrote to them about the happy days they had spent with their master Lucinius ("dear fellow Lucinian"). Arius appealed to friendship and the *elan* of a scholarly elite.

Locally, he wrote to his fellow Miletians, commending them for never having lowered their standards even when they were put down publicly. Former Miletians liked the sound of this: they had not lost, they had shown their fortitude.

As Arius belabored the bishops who had put down the Miletianism, former Miletians rallied to him. The rallying relied on friendship, unrequited anger about early defeats, and petty ecclesiastical alliances. No doubt, some of these people entertained doubts about Christ's unqualified divinity, but the fuel of the dispute was overwhelming party spirit and the desire to unseat those who had triumphed in an earlier quarrel.

It is impossible to understand the lunar tides of this controversy without understanding the Roman Empire. Those who approach the question with perceptions of a later national state or with medieval models will never comprehend the context of the dispute.

The Roman Empire was not a government or state by any modern definition. Contemporaries thought of the Empire as an awesome, almost incredible, and perhaps miraculous intervention in history. Pagan piety explained it as a divine arrangement. The irreligious were not less pious regarding its accomplishments. In a world entirely used to unending warlord violence, endemic banditry and piracy, the termination of internal strife and peril astonished everyone. It delighted those who loved family, property, commerce, scholarship, art, travel and any civilized accomplishment. Brutality existed, but it largely preserved the peace.

The Imperial principle defined true civilization in the only form 4th century people could conceive of it. Roman law begins with the protection of the state. Imperialists would have been shocked by any other suggestion. That one man's rights might challenge the effective guardianship of all civilized living was considered too foolish for consideration. Civilization and the safety of the Empire was co-terminous. Defying or harming the Empire was for all Roman citizens unthinkable.

Into this world entered Constantine. He had the required qualifications for Imperial office. He was a known professional soldier whose duty of protecting the borders of the Empire had been nicely fulfilled. And he had an army.

Constantine was also highly intelligent. He understood the political traffic and never doubted for a moment the final success for any venture to which he turned his hand. His personal religion centered on a lesser known devotion to *Sol Invictor,* which he revived and established as soon as his power was secure. Happily, *Sol Invictor* was a *summa deus,* and Constantine was at home with the one and only God.

At the same time, he was generally converted to Christianity and fancied himself a messenger of Christ. This was one more reminder of his good instinct for victory. Moreover, The Edict of Milan was the work of an honest admirer of Christianity and an astute constitutional thinker acting cautiously as he liberated the Christians from persecution.

When the Emperor dealt with heretical Donatistism, he discovered an effective instrument of government. He discovered a Council of Bishops that met to resolve problems. He liked that. It was very Roman, very manageable.

He entered into the problems of the Church as a true friend of Christian ideals, but he remained wholly innocent of theology and Christian absolutes. His intrusion into Church affairs was not considered strange or unbecoming according to the perceptions of the day.

When the Catholic bishops found they could not resolve the Arian theological questions by persuasion nor by episcopal authority, and the divisions turned genuinely disruptive of community peace, degenerating into a violence that obscured proper authority, Constantine turned to a bishops' council as the obvious first step. He summoned the Council of Nicea and protested that he was not there to manage the Council. He only half-heartedly meant that, but, fortunately, the strong-minded people who attended the Council did what the Emperor hoped they would. He assumed he was to confirm the Council somehow and stood by to enforce it. He expected his magistrates to enforce religious orthodoxy as a form of good civil order.

The Emperor Constantine's interest in the Arian-Catholic debate transformed the basic terms of the conflict. It did not transform the terms of the theological debates: they were to elemental. But the terms of the conflict and the way in which it was conducted were radically changed by Imperial intervention.

I will not offend this group with a definition of the Arian controversy and how it forced forward a question that had to be faced sooner or later — namely, a definition in Greek and Latin words that would lime and protect the mystery of the Incarnation and the divinity of Christ. In this regard, every thinking Catholic cherishes the name of Athanasius whose doubtful tomb in the Venetian Church of Santa Zaccaria we venerate for lack of a better one. With Athanasius and others at work, the age was hardly a theological loss, for there were problems that threatened basic theological processes.

The trouble began when, as we noted above, the affable and more than competent Bishop Alexander of Alexandria made a misappraisal of a disaffected priest. Arius, the priest, did not take lightly the disgrace and suppression of the Miletian position on which he had pinned his ecclesiastical hopes. The nicely educated, generous-minded Alexander thought to bring Arius, a bright fellow, back into the Alexandrine church family. Arius was hardly desirous of reconciliation. He began preaching a doctrine he knew was far more disturbing than any view on the *lapsi* or re-baptism. His early and later history suggest he abhorred those in power and challenged their orthodoxy largely because it was theirs.

Having rallied the Miletian alumni and his old school friends, Arius went off to Palestine just ahead of his ex-communication in Alexandria. At Palestine, he secured the backing of a prominent theologian, Eusebius, Bishop of Caesarea, who promptly joined Arius in circularizing the bishops of the world. With many lightly paid copyists, their system of communication was excellent. It did service for the contemporary

11:00 news, an annual subscription to USSC publications and the steam room of the local clerical gym. The system was lively and highly articulate.

Eusebius of Caesarea was a good, honorable and courageous bishop. He wrote to Alexander saying that perhaps Alexander misunderstood and misjudged Arius and his followers who would, by that misunderstanding, be driven to extremes. Eusebius also joined the Syrian bishops in suggesting that Arius be freed of his Alexandrine excommunication, while admonishing Arius to obey his bishop in peace. A very episcopal observation! But the bishops were as innocent of Arius' real temperament as Alexander had been earlier.

Arius had not mistaken Eusebius' prestige. At Nicea, Eusebius sat on Constantine's right hand and had high hopes of keeping open all options. He spoke for a bland, non-judgmental formula. When the Council voted for a clear and decisively Catholic formulation, Eusebius signed what he knew to be true if "inopportune" (as the word would be used later). Nicea was a blow to Arius; but Eusebius consoled him by spending the rest of his life, about 15 years, trying to stretch the unyielding words of Nicea to cover Arian teaching. Happily, Eusebius is remembered more for his love of the martyrs and his histories. But Arius used Eusebius' hospitality to raise his own reputation among his Lucinian fellow alumni. His future would be intimately connected with a fellow Lucinian, another Eusebius, Eusebius of Nicomedia, the true creator of the Arian party that would long outlive Arius.

Indeed it was the Eusebian party henceforth that promoted Arianism. It is the judgment of most careful historians that Arianism, a set of theological propositions that pre-dated Arius, was from the moment Arius promoted it, through Eusebius of Caesarea's attempt to protect it and Eusebius of Nicomedia's leadership, a matter of ecclesiastical and imperial intrigue throughout. Its theological conjugation took place in a context of such overpowering partisan attempts to replace Catholic bishops by imperial intervention and patronage that the test of a cleric's position was rarely cogency or theological authority — it was throughout, loyalty and power.

Consider the hunt for power by Eusebius of Nicomedia. He secured a second diocese and left his first despite a strong, normative ban on changing dioceses, precisely because he wished to secure the diocese in which the Eastern Emperor resided.

At Nicea, Eusebius of Nicomedia's Arian proposal secured only 17 out of 300 votes. His speeches were hooted down as beyond consideration. Smugly, he signed the voted creed which manifestly rejected

Arianism, but he refused then to condemn Arianism. This remains a remarkable sign of how little he was interested in theological process. Eusebius of Nicomedia said disingenuously that Arius had been misinterpreted. How often we will hear that in history.

He and Arius were banished for two years. But even in this period he did not give up intrigue. Constantia, the widow of the former Emperor, pleaded with the Emperor for Arius and Eusebius and, after the two years, they were permitted to return, mumbling orthodox phrases to permit passage home, but wholly unchanged. They were more than ever determined to secure through the Imperial court what power Nicea had denied them.

Four years after Nicea, Eusebius was once more in high personal favor with the Emperor. He had a number of admirers. They too were wholly oriented toward the acquisition of power. Athanasius named these late first generation Arians "Eusebians," and saw them, correctly, as setting out to undo Nicea. Cleverly, to please the Emperor, they became spokesmen for the largest body of bishops in Constantinople, loudly venerating Lucian as a martyr and Origen as a great thinker, and did not advert to the fact that they drew from each quiet confirmation of their Arian views. They simply dropped the Nicean creed without comment, spoke ambiguously, and warned everyone against the extremes of Sabellianism in which the distinction of divine persons in the trinity was obscured.

Strong anti-Arian bishops were deposed by Imperial order on the word of the Eusebians who called the bishops Sabellians. Others were removed for various reasons like failing to show proper respect for the Emperor's mother. Others were charged gratuitously with immorality. Eusebius had at his disposal Imperial power, and he used it ruthlessly.

Athanasius succeeded Alexander in the See of Alexandria the year before Eusebius regained his power in Constantinople. He had the solid support of 100 Alexandrine bishops. He was clearly Eusebius' main enemy. The Eusebians talked the Emperor Constantine into writing a letter to Athanasius ordering him to receive back into communion both Arians and Miletians. Eusebius failed when Athanasius answered firmly in the negative and the Emperor backed off. Theological dialogue of any meaning did not enter this maneuver, even though Athanasius articulated his case well. Theology was simply not the subject.

We will not have space here to catalogue the openly mendacious charges, from magic to treason, made against Athanasius by the Eusebians. Those charges led to four exiles, underlining for every generation Athanasius' integrity, fortitude and resilience in his fight for orthodoxy in the matter of Christ's divinity. Eusebius orchestrated the unrelenting assaults on Athanasius' character; manipulated Athanasius' old enemies into actions, sometimes violent; and repeatedly won Imperial consent to exile Athanasius through all manner of deception. Cardinal Newman's lament that the most damage the Church suffers ecclesiastically comes from party spirit was exemplified perfectly by Eusebius.

Eusebius used every device he could think of. At one synod (Tyre, 335), he systematically excluded all supporters of Athanasius and then orchestrated the synod to condemn Athanasius and remand him to jail. Athanasius barely escaped. By threatening all Catholic bishops with jail, Eusebius cleared the area and was able — with a rump synod — to rehabilitate Arius ecclesiastically.

At Constantinople, Eusebius controlled which bishops could enter the city and approach the Emperor. When the Emperor decided that Athanasius was probably innocent of all charges, the Eusebians stated, without a blush, that Athanasius had threatened to hold up grain shipments from Alexandria to Constantinople — a matter of life and death for the Imperial City. An enraged Emperor immediately exiled Athanasius without investigation. These were purely political triumphs through intrigue. Theology was talked constantly, but it had no serious role in the events of the day.

When the Miletian leaders were no longer useful to Eusebius, he had them banished as well. Such successful intrigue touching the whole known world has rarely been matched in history. Throughout the East, almost all pro-Nicean bishops were deposed.

Eusebius even captured the trust of Constantine's successor in the East — Constantius. And, indeed, the damaging intrigues of the Eusebians continued throughout the century long after the death of Eusebius in 341. He died as Archbishop of Constantinople, his third See. A worldly prelate, he created, by untiring party activity, outrageous lying, and the use of civil power, a pattern that would be imitated by many in the centuries that followed. He established that theology can be placed almost entirely in the service of power and that theological controversy can be so directed as to make the emergence of unshadowed truth barely possible. Eusebius of Nicomedia also represents the first prelate to dedicate himself to the unqualified use of political power to silence ecclesiastical rivals. He further proved that bishops, priests, and their followers can be rallied into parties whose consuming passion, at least for a time, is the destruction of their opponent's positions of influence, their good name, and their ministry.

My thesis is that only a theologian of heroic dedication to the truth could have weathered such pressures and continued true theological work. Athanasius did precisely that, and that is why he remains a towering figure in Christian history. But even here, surely the largest part of his time was spent in fending off the intrigues of his enemies.

The Fratacelli or Spiritual Franciscans

The Fratacelli were followers of Saint Francis of Assisi who required of all Franciscans, among other demands, absolute poverty. They were not one group, but many pockets of strong-minded Franciscans. They were also called Spiritual Franciscans or Spirituals. The Fratacelli nicknamed the main line Franciscans or Conventuals the *"relaxati."* Italian literature sometimes uses the word "Fratacelli" to refer to all manner of friars and solitaries. But we use the term here to refer only to the dissenting Franciscans of the 13th and 14th centuries.

St. Francis practiced comprehensive poverty without clearly requiring it of his associates. In the late 13th century, as the number of Franciscans exploded across Christendom, the management of large convents and of provinces made absolute and strict communal poverty practically impossible. Absolute poverty was always possible for individuals, however much the practitioners may have annoyed their associates.

If the problem had remained an intra-Franciscan debate or war, it would not draw our attention in this paper. In fact, the division rattled the lives of a considerable part of the Christian community, drove the Holy See to divided counsels, involved heresy, and threatened schism.

An early group of pro-absolute poverty enthusiasts was inspired by Fra Angelo da Clareno who, in his career, reflected the Church's confusion. In 1278, he was condemned and imprisoned for extreme views, then paroled and exiled, then re-commissioned as a missionary, then called back into personal favor by the ascetic six-month Pope Celestine V, then banished again, and finally tolerated as he established an illegal community of Friars, who he said were the real Friars Minor. By the late 13th century, the strongest passions had been aroused among most Franciscans and also in curias in whose territories the Franciscan quarrels occurred. Nor were the Dominicans happy about "uneducated Franciscans" defining what a friar ought to be.

When passions regarding basic identity are current, every movement and countermovement, however slight, can create new dangerous situations. And so it was. In a gesture of reconciliation, Nicholas III (1279) attempted (in the Bull **Exiit qui seminat**) to interpret and even justify the best aspects of the Fratacelli mind. This piece of generous-mindedness provoked the Conventual Franciscans into strong repressive measures against the Fratacelli who, after decades of alienation, forcibly seized several monasteries in central Italy. Local Archbishops moved against them. About 55 Fratacelli fled to Sicily and sought royal protection. In these alarming circumstances the Holy See (1314) ex-communicated the offending friars and interdicted the seized monasteries. Now most of the Fratacelli fled to Sicily.

The dispute became more intense when respected Augustinian hermits and well-known writers on the spiritual life, like Gentile da Foligno and Simone de Cassia, defended Fratacelli views. The question was now openly debated on a theological level, as well as canonical and popular levels.

The rebellious friars issued a solemn protest (1313) full of theological and legal reasoning against their repression by the Holy See. Their most active spokesman was Enrico da Ceva. His main theological points are described in the Bull that condemned the Fratacelli (Pope John XXII: **"Glosiosam ecclesiam,"** January, 1318) — namely: (1) the known Catholic Church had been corrupted and, on principle, puts carnal material matters before the spiritual and thereby ceases to follow the Gospel; (2) the contemporary priesthood that functions under the alleged Papal jurisdiction is without power; (3) any priest in a state of sin cannot confer the sacraments validly; and (4) only the Fratacelli are the true followers of Christ and his Gospel. It is what will be called later the *petite eglise* mentality, an elitest church within the larger body of corrupted or misled believers.

At this time, the Fratacelli considered their immediate enemy not the Pope but the Conventual Franciscans, whose convents they had seized. Secondarily, they feared the local bishop commissioned by the Pope to tag and suppress the heresy. Fratacelli theologians responded to threats by supplying Scriptural and scholarly materials to help dilute or reject the Pope's jurisdiction. But they went beyond that saying that all priests and religious who reject the equation of absolute poverty and Christ's message were damned. To clear the board, they pleaded that such priests, and any priest who committed a mortal sin, were deprived of their dignity and power. It is, perhaps, self-serving to my thesis to call all these advocates theologians. But they talked theology. Their purposes were manifestly advocacy, perhaps touched by fear. From their rejection of what they considered an intolerable interpretation of Scripture (namely, that Christ did not choose total poverty), they reasoned to the thought that so sinful a misuse of Christ's message must damn, remove, and banish their ecclesiastical persecutors. There is no reason to challenge their sincerity. Indeed, there were saints among them. Even a miracle-worker or two.

To find a solution to such ghastly divisions through Christendom, Pope John XXII turned, desparately perhaps, not to his own theologians nor to Inquisitors, nor to Conventual theologians, but to a renowned writer among the Fratacelli, Ubertino of Casale. Ubertino developed a hair-splitting distinction: namely, that Christ and the Apostles owned property as governors of the Church but not as individuals or as witnesses to Christian virtue. Exhausted combatants and a weary Papal Curia cozied up to that pathetic legal fiction hoping for a solution to the seemingly irreducible conflict between theology and the interests of time. Happily or unhappily for theology, the dilemma was resolved by a preemptive strike of Michael of Cesena, the minster general of the Conventual Franciscans. He led a general chapter of the Franciscans (June 1322) in proclaiming the "absolute poverty of Christ" and published the pronouncement to Christendom. Furious, Pope John XXII reacted sharply, perhaps overreacted, and abolished Franciscan poverty altogether and returned to the Franciscans all the properties held in their behalf by the Holy See. Practically speaking, he abolished Franciscan identity. The following year, Cesena's views of Christ's poverty were declared heretical by the Pope. Anticipating a later development, a respected Conventual canonist, Fra Boncortese Bonagrazia, appealed from the Pope to the consistory that the Pope had summoned to review these questions.

Sensing that the ground on which they stood was not secure, most of the Fratacelli moved swiftly to Sicily and sought the protection of a baron, King Robert.

The views of the Fratacelli won theological respect mainly in the work of Michael of Cesena. His followers took the name "Michaelites." He distinguished the pragmatic controversy within the Franciscan community about the degree of poverty to be observed by Franciscans. Here the opponents were implacable enemies. Against this, Cesena posed a second controversy, more theoretical than the first, about the nature of poverty in Christ's life, and, reflectively, in Franciscan and general Christian life. In this controversy, he felt he and his brothers led the battle against Pope John XXII for the sake of all Franciscans.

Lines crossed. Cesena found strength by associating his preaching with the mysticism of the Beghards, already corrupted by a proto-Quietism and repeatedly condemned by the Holy See. Fratacelli-Beghard mysticism drifted rapidly into Gnostic modes and into anarchistic lifestyles. When Dominican preachers and Inquisitors moved against them, the division took on an inter-community battle, Dominicans versus Franciscans. But even the rally against the Dominicans did not unite the Franciscans.

Who is to say what Cesena's final values were? It is conceivable that he and his associates thought of their theology largely as a tool of survival in battle. Consider their situation. They were battling against the majority of their fellow Franciscans, condemning them as ascetically and spiritually corrupt. They were fending off Inquisitorial and prejudiced Dominicans. They were condemned by the Holy See and required as a party to justify a rejection of the visible Papacy. At the same time, the Michaelites declared invalid the sacraments conferred by doubtful clerics; preached a hitherto hidden mandate of Christ for total poverty; encouraged a Quietistic mysticism; and justified violent action in the name of Christ. Is it not reasonable to say that this man and his associates were hardly in a position to pursue theological truth dispassionately or even credibly?

Consider the equally unsettled situation of their opponents, the Popes. In 1245, Pope Nicholas III gave Papal solace to the Fratacelli (Exiit qui seminat). He spoke of the individual and corporate poverty of the Franciscans as "equivalent" to that of the Apostles and, in token of that thought, transferred possession of all Franciscan lands and houses to the Apostolic See where they were held in custody for the Franciscans. He then imposed a silence on the question of Apostolic poverty, a legal fiction ignored by the dissenters. By the early 1300's, several Popes and Inquisitors, with their theological back-up teams, had roundly condemned the unsound Fratacelli position regarding Christ's poverty and His alleged injunction for absolute poverty. Seventy-seven years after Nicholas' Bull, Pope John XXII formally lifted Nicholas' silence and convoked a consistory on the subject.

Consider the context in which even theoretically neutral theologians and canonists had to work. A Franciscan-Dominican standoff froze the question in most academic and professional circles, and dulled — if not paralyzed — theological exchange.

Is it cynical to think that with so many furies loose in the land, serious scholarship regarding the mind of Christ and the practice of the Apostles, along with ascetical questions of poverty, were not likely to receive the benefits of indifferent study? Theologians were enlisted, almost impressed, into one of three or four major positions, and their conclusions were passionately sought by dozens of groups of Franciscans. Objective scholarship was not impossible, but consider the magnetic fields created by these honest contemporary Franciscan passions: (1) a powerful determination to protect the essential ideals of

St. Francis, an ideal that had already reformed the spiritual lives of millions of people with eminent success; (2) a powerful determination to keep pure the verified ascetical ideal of total detachment from material things for those capable of it; (3) a desire to shore up that ideal by finding roots of it in Christ's practice; (4) the need to protect popular Franciscan institutions throughout Christendom; and (5) a justified fear of anarchism, frequently violent and sadistic.

On the other side, consider the following needs of Papal and non-Franciscan theologians and canonists: (1) to protect Papal jurisdiction and popular confidence in sacramental ministry; (2) to keep the Conventual Franciscans free of Fratacelli domination; (3) to keep a rescue line out to sincere Fratacelli; (4) to keep the Franciscans loyal to the Holy See despite 95 degree turns from one Papal Bull to another, as, e.g., from early Papal condemnations to Celestine V's personal encouragement of the Fratacelli and Nicholas III's pro-poverty position to John XXII's hunt for compromise and his final extreme anti-poverty position; (5) to prevent predatory princes and prejudiced Dominicans from crushing Franciscan institutions. All these were honest needs and everyone of them, Franciscan and non-Franciscan, a magnet pulling scholars away from the theological subjects before them, such as questions regarding the mind of Christ and the Apostles, the parameters of sound mysticism, and the definition of poverty of spirit and life. The direct pressures on theologians from forces pulling them from profitable inquiries were both strong and, in certain ways, necessary and justifiable in the context of the day. Scholars must have despaired privately of objective discussion and thought they were writing for another age. How many of the published works of the time made a serious contribution to the development of Christian thinking? Not many. Did partisan battles contribute to the development of Christian thought? Obliquely, they did as they always do. But extreme positions and unsound views leap out at us and they sweep away theses that, for literate people, need not be debated again. That is no small contribution to the development of doctrine — paid for by the passion, pain and suffering of so many partisans and other good men and women who had to hope for better times.

Conclusion

Consider how many other struggles illustrate our points. Conciliarism, the Lutheran rebellion and the Calvinist revolution, the furious battles over Grace, Jansenism, the blows of the Enlightenment and then theological Liberalism — to name only the largest struggles.

Let us look for a moment at 1985. Whole circles of allegedly theological activity chill the work of scholarship. Consider just a few.

How many thousands rejoice in the mock-theology of the feminist movement within the Catholic Church! In public debate, the phrases of pop psychology are put forward as Christian verities. Scripture, the history of the papacy, and the history of religious communities are cited wrecklessly. The feminist movement is a political campaign thinly disguised as a theological imperative.

How Tertullian would have leaped from his chair to hear the Women's Ordination Conference on March 5, 1985 say, to the Bishops, in a parable:

> ... the temple itself was in great tumult and confusion. Over centuries it had come to pass that the high priests only were allowed to make policy, determine budgets, and conduct the sacred rites of the temple. Those rites were called sacraments. And to be a high priest, one must not only be a man, but a man who would promise never to love a woman in marriage. A man, thus distanced from and renouncing women, became a high priest through the ritual called Ordination.
>
> Now the high priests claimed all this as God's will because it had always been so. (**Origins,** Vol. 14, No. 40, page 659)

Many also speak as if a consensus existed from Apostolic times that the goal of Christian revelation is the extirpation of poverty, racial discrimination, and war.

Also, millions of our people believe today that the ministries of the Church are chiefly aids to psychological contentment and worldly success. Consequently, they are appalled by the suggestion that they should not choose those sacraments and doctrines that please them and reject those that do not. For them and for the up-coming generation still taught by kindly secularists in Catholic schools, the concept of authority in the teaching of religion is ludicrous. Nor do they think that their source is different from what all Catholics have ever believed down the ages.

We should say a scholar can barely function in such a scene. Yet such opinions are held by known presidents of universities and heads of theology departments, and it is impossible to ignore them.

In several major religious communities, a Holy War is spoken of as a Christian opportunity whenever no other solution is perceived for poverty. Scripture is cited. Sometimes the same people call for total pacifism. Scripture is also cited. Where does a scholar begin?

What an elevated Catholic mind it is that can look at the poorly framed questions of an age and respond empathetically; that can try to speak wisdom against the noisy demands of the moment; that can drift back intellectually and spiritually to moments in history when minds were freer; that can reach into another culture where questions are construed differently; that can consider imaginatively the near future freed of today's priorities and open to fresh insights.

Such scholars fill us with awe. They are at home with the truth and the virtue of Christ, and rise to that freedom Christ promised us in the Gospel of St. John:

> And now Jesus said to those among the Jews who believed in Him, 'If you continue faithful to my word, you are my disciples in earnest; so you will come to know the truth, and the truth will set you free'
> (John 8:31-33)

We know what *can* be done, because it *has* been done so often in history:

— by Augustine, writing with intellectual detachment as the Roman Empire and all civilization as he knew it was being extinguished around him;

— by Athanasius, the indestructible hero of all truth-lovers;

— by Abelard, against so many, insisting upon the untrammeled use of the intellect;

— by Aquinas, drawing into the service of Christian thinking unspeakable integrity;

— by Cajetan, as the furies howled around him, speaking so carefully;

— by Francis de Sales, ignoring a vicious age and telling the laity of the joys of the ascetical life and sanctity;

— by our inimitable Newman, confronting the mountain slide of liberalism, putting his injuries aside, as he sifted history and theology for pure gold.

The passions of the age, intimidation, the kettle drums of argument, are nearly silenced for scholars who can say and mean:

> Veni, Creator Spiritus,
> Mentes tuorum visita,
> Imple superna gratia
> Qua Tu creasti pectora.

The First Draft of the
Bishops' Pastoral Letter on the Economy

by

Regis A. Factor

The Bishops' Draft Letter on the Economy reflects developments in the Catholic Church in America and developments in American society. Neither of these is especially salutary. The deviations from Catholic teaching continue trends expressed in previous statements of American clergy, religious, and in the Bishops' Pastoral Letter on War and Peace, and constitute in certain ways an attack on the authentic teaching authority of the Church. It is the purpose of this paper to furnish a critique of the Bishops' Letter on the Economy, focusing principally on the weaknesses of the document. Unfortunately, this approach does not do justice to the many segments which reflect the teaching of the Church. In this sense, the paper is necessarily incomplete as it only strives to bring the document into line with Church teaching.

The Church's teaching on economics has been incorporated in its social teachings. Economic structures and economic policies are subordinated to the common good, which itself recognizes the spiritual realm or spiritual dimension as primary over the material one. The worker is not a commodity but is viewed in his personhood, in his bond with eternal life, and in his relationships with his family, his country, and the peoples of the world. Labor rightly asserts its primacy over capital. Neither "pure" socialism nor "pure" capitalism constitutes the "correct" economic order, for human freedom must be given its due while human imperfections must be recognized and addressed.

The Bishops examine initially the perspectives on the economy derived from the revealed truths of scripture, or, to be more precise, on the biblical principles which should be applied to animate economic life with the spirit of Christ. Some relationships described in this section would benefit from modification, such as the comment that we are to "realize that people of other nations ... should be equal recipients of God's bounty." [1] At various times in the Bishops' letter, an egalitarian perspective intrudes which injures basic principles of the Church's social teaching. In this instance, it is the demand that the redistribution of wealth be conducted on a scale to achieve equal possession "of God's bounty." The principles which are to permeate living in a country (i.e., truth, justice, love and liberty) are not served by the overemphasizing of an egalitarian principle of this character. The Church recognizes the principle that, within proper limits, one is entitled to the fruit of one's labor.

The letter, somewhat surprisingly, attaches primacy to the idea of justice [2] in the theological reflection on economic matters, while the principle of love plays a subordinate role. Without diminishing the significance of justice, one nevertheless must insist on elevating the principle of love, which would strengthen the document and avoid difficulties in subsequent sections, the chief of which being the overemphasis upon the material needs of the poor and the lesser emphasis on their spiritual needs — for love is the definitive source of everything that exists. In the authors' pursuit of consensus, the claim that "laws are just when they create harmony within the community" is simply erroneous.[3] To affirm this can lead one to accept artificial contraception, since most American Catholics support it and often become distressed when told that its practice is immoral. The Church does not follow the wishes of the majority. Its function is not to seek popularity nor to sacrifice truth to expediency or for the sake of harmony.

The omission of mention of the nature of the family and its role as the basic unit of society is a serious oversight, as well as the lack of any reference, especially since the letter is addressed to the American people, to the brutal onslaught on the lives of the unborn and other defenseless members of our society. The section dealing with the ethical norms or with those norms derived from Catholic social principles which are designed to guide Americans in the economic realm also lacks the enrichment which would result from the inclusion of the above.

This section of the document is fraught with numerous difficulties as basic social principles are here incorrectly defined or wrongly applied. Chief among these is the confusion about the teaching principles of the Church. This confusion is especially injurious since the latter section concerning policy implications is rendered even more disconcerting and uncertain. Here is where the egalitarian principle is strikingly present. In the form used, it diminishes the concern for the spiritual well-being of the people and overstresses the significance of material progress. The contrast with Pope John Paul's encyclical letter, "On Human Work," [4] is manifest. In that letter, work or labor is highlighted as "a sharing in the activity of the Creator" [5] and is a noble activity.

The Bishops advocate the creation of an economic democracy, the purpose of which is to guarantee "the minimum conditions of human dignity in the economic sphere for every person." [6]

The attainment of this order is the result of a moral enlightenment and the institution of particular institutional processes and procedures. The establishment of these techniques or institutional arrangements becomes an ethical demand in itself. The merits of political participation as claimed by theorists of interest group activity imbues this teaching. The tradition continuing down to our time from Adam Smith, whose economic views are vehemently attacked in this document, is paradoxically affirmed in some of its assumptions.

Justice "demands the establishment of minimum levels of participation by all persons in the life of the human community." [7] The "most urgent demand of justice" is to overcome the "powerlessness" of people.[8] The lack of political power is viewed as most improper, and the Bishops clearly advocate redistributing power.[9] Social institutions are "to be ordered in a way that guarantees all persons the ability to participate actively in the economic, political, and cultural life of the community." [10] The idea of being concerned with the well-being of every member of our nation is laudable, but to insist that national well-being is only possible via participation in decision-making by every member in the political and economic spheres is stretching the scope of the ethical norm. Justice, they continue, flows from power. As such, justice requires the progress toward a democratic society. Moreover, they maintain that proper distribution of economic wealth requires democracy. They mention that Pope Paul VI in his advocacy of political society meant democratic society.[11] And so, the Bishops conclude, greater participation suggests more moral results. But this is not correct. Majority rule does not always lead to greater justice, nor do the Popes say that the democratic society is more spiritually fulfilling than other political forms. Pope John XXIII did not say that the democratic regime was a superior form, although translators of **Pacem in terris** so claimed in their translations. If this idea were true, it would denigrate all those people who live or have lived under non-democratic regimes and all those rulers who actually promoted the common good in the exercise of their authority.

The principle of subsidiarity suffers under the same burden as justice as it is now said to guarantee "institutional pluralism." [12] The Church does not advocate the necessity of implementing political pluralism; democratic ideologists and prudential politicians do. As one might have expected or feared, the institutional Church itself is now told to "democratize" itself.[13] The Church is described as a "sinful human community." [14] Whether or not this description is corrected by subsequent remarks does not assuage the fact that such a comment does not belong in this document. Certainly, some American priests and theologians have insisted on democratic or "aristocratic" rule in the Church, but Christ gave the authentic teaching authority to the Church, not to an American community of theologians or to an American Catholic consensus. The principles of the common good and prudence need to be introduced and integrated in various sections for the sake of clarity and to avoid misunderstanding. Without them, the fulfillment of a citizen's responsibilities and the proper expression of liberty is less likely. The emphasis in the letter on action, active behavior, and dynamism tends to indicate that these qualities are good in themselves, when, in actuality, patience, silence, and moderation might be required in given circumstances. There is little mention of the value of contemplation and meditation, and one is said to need "interaction, interdependence, communication, and collaboration" to "grow to full self-realization." [15] Priests and nuns in contemplative orders seemingly fail to meet the demands of dynamism and activism and thus cannot actualize themselves.

In the description of community, the extensive reliance on the idea of "solidarity" is misplaced since, as Pope John XXIII expressed in **Pacem in terris,** "solidarity" is a principle employed in characterizing proper relations among nations, not among citizens of the same country. The correct principle that should be employed to describe relations among citizens of the same country is that of love. The failure to recognize this teaching hampered the argument of the Bishops' Pastoral Letter on War and Peace and also harms this document, for what it essentially does, as the Bishops employ the principle of solidarity, is to weaken the obligations a citizen has to his own country. As the obligation to care for other people is now equal to the care for one's own fellow citizens and family, a citizen loses his proper understanding of duty to country and family. Moreover, by reducing the concern for one's fellow citizens from that of love to solidarity, one negates the true importance of one's national community.

A discussion of employment and of the economy has to address the problems of the beleaguered family. Yet there is no investigation of the different roles of parents and of their separate missions other than to equate those roles under the rubric of equal rights. Pope John Paul II has reminded us of the special role of the mother as nurturer for her children and that women as mothers have an irreplaceable role.

Quite naturally, the letter concentrates on alleviating poverty, something which all of us have to strive to eliminate. In the key passage dealing with poverty, the Bishops explain:

> Poverty is not merely the lack of adequate financial resources. To be poor entails a more profound kind of deprivation, for it means being denied *full participation* [my italics] in the economic, social, and political life of society. It means being without sufficient control over and access to the

decisions that affect your life. It means being marginalized and powerless in a way that assaults not only your pocketbook but also your fundamental human dignity.[16]

In the above quotation, it is difficult not to conclude that one in poverty has been severely harmed in his deepest being, in his dignity, in his soul. Is a poor person so harmed? We have all known or read about financially poor people of exemplary dignity and admirable qualities of character. They are not as deprived or degraded as those who fail to aid them. One is at the mercy of the economic and social order, according to the Bishops, and no genuinely human response is possible by those who are powerless. Again, they say, being poor is almost a sin, a social sin perhaps, and a theology of liberation is required for secular triumph.

Should St. Francis of Assisi have devoted himself to a democratic revolution, insisting that he have access to governmental decision-making, and have worried about the degrading sense of his political powerlessness? Did this factor hinder or prevent his self-actualization? Of course not. In their concern for helping the poor, who very much need our love and charity, the Bishops have stumbled into a political conception which is derived not from Church teaching but from those who opposed or ignored the Church. The pursuit and the acquisition of power play too prominent a place in this document and are more suited to the interest group political theory of contemporary ideologists. In this theory, there is too little place for a genuine conception of the common good, and that may explain its infrequent appearances.

It is therefore not surprising to read in this letter that Pope John Paul II is alleged to be calling us "to seek that balance between individual initiatives and the common good which is the responsibility of all citizens." [17] This statement is incorrect for a number of reasons. It "seeks" to create a conflict or dissonance between individual initiative or interest and the common interest when what is involved is rather a conception of the common good which transcends interests and comprehends the goods of all. Nothing is "balanced" with the common good since, by its nature, any "balancing" is excluded. The Popes have continuously stated that individuals are to be restrained when the common good so requires, and that the principle of subsidiarity applies.

In the section in which the Bishops offer their exhortations for re-shaping the economy, greater participation is expectedly emphasized.[18] In the extensive examination of global economic relationships, the richer countries are exhorted to help the less-developed countries (LDC), while the LDC are to insist upon greater roles (i.e., participation in decisions). Greater use of international organizations is strongly encouraged, and the bilateral approach is criticized. What the Bishops should have cautioned is that international organizations be granted additional responsibility in those circumstances in which the common good is likely served. Bilateral aid may at various times be a better means to serve peoples. The principle of subsidiarity also applies to the question of determining how much authority should be granted to an international authority. Certainly, increasing the authority of international governmental structures is not a good in itself.

The primary focus in the U. S. and relationships with other countries should be the salvation of souls and feeding those souls, not economic redistribution.[19] In this section of the text, the theme of interest appears this time in the form of an appeal to national interest. I quote:

> As a nation founded on Judeo-Christian religious principles, we are called to make those sacrifices in order to bring justice and peace to the world, as well as for our own long-term self-interest. [20]

The principle of self-interest may be appealing or persuasive to those not motivated by good will, but the Church has always rejected it as a principle of action, and it should be excised from this document. The Bishops' Letter perpetuates errors that appeared in their recent letter dealing with war and peace.[21] In that pastoral document, one encounters erroneous presentations of the concept of justice and of the value of pluralist democracy, along with a negation of patriotism and the plea for agreement on the basis of coincidence of interests.[22] As it has been explained to me, that document contains many divergent views expressed in the contemporary American Catholic Church. Should Americans hear the Church speaking with several voices? I think not. The magisterium speaks with one voice and it deserves a privileged place.

United States policies are vehemently attacked. Many of the criticisms are accurate; some are not. It should be recalled that no nation ever dealt with weaker nations as generously as the United States has in this century. The document lists a litany of criticisms of the United States which present an incomplete or distorted picture. Even United Nations studies indicate that there is not a basic shortage of material resources. It is not evident that multilateral aid is superior to bilateral aid. We are accused of failing to sign the Genocide Convention. Yet we have done more to assist the targets of genocide than any other country. The theory of economic dependency introduced by the Bishops has been widely rejected by contemporary economists. There exists in their letter confusion in describing the relationship between terms of trade and exports/imports. Moreover, the failures of third world leadership are insufficiently presented, as are various other factors restricting the growth of less-developed countries.

In summary, the Bishops' letter needs to include a discussion of the family and would benefit from examining the problem of the economy from a perspective imbued by the spirit and substance of Pope John Paul II's encyclical letter on work. This would enable them to avoid the intimation that individual rights practically eclipse the rights of the family, and to escape a somewhat materialist view of workers and workers' needs. Without the primacy of the spiritual realm, it becomes facile to insist on the transformation of social and economic structures via the seizure of political power. Liberation is thus viewed as resulting from the conquest of power.

In buttressing their arguments, the Bishops' reliance on non- or anti-Catholic sources has led them to accept other tenets of those writers' thinking and the ultimate loss of aspects of the Catholic doctrinal treasure. At times, it appears that the Bishops have adopted sections of the Democratic Party platform. These restrictive economic policies have not worked. The letter seems oblivious to the so-called "supply-side" revolution in economics. There may be deficiencies in the supply-side perspective, but to ignore that challenge is difficult to comprehend. Instead, they choose to oppose only monetarism, which is certainly an adversary much easier to overcome. An ennobled conception of patriotism and love of country needs to be added, along with a proper emphasis on the common good and on the virtue of prudence. Americans must be called on to fight the abortion and contraceptive mentality, divorce and pornography, and to reintroduce the notion of personal responsibility and personal sin. The Bishops are correct when they stress that America is suffering under a "crisis of citizenship." [23] Unfortunately, they have not availed themselves of the opportunity to proclaim that inspirational theory of citizenship for which our country sorely yearns.

Perhaps the most serious problem in the letter is the misrepresentation of Catholic social teaching as to what constitutes ethical norms. It appears that this was discarded in order to introduce certain egalitarian ideas (e.g., pluralism, etc., which derive from a liberal notion of human nature and a faith in democracy and dialogue which augment or replace the official teaching of the Church). Does Catholic America represent Catholicism "coming of age" as a recent article states? [24] Or does it represent the vanguard of the universal Roman Church? The infatuation with certain "American things, ideas" has led to an inflated view of ourselves as being "ahead of Rome." This is not really even a democratic outlook. It is a view of self-adulation, of a claimed superiority, a view which does not recognize the duty to obey, nor to shepherd the American Catholic flock in correspondence with Christ's teaching. To adhere to that duty may lead to a loss of popularity, to the charge of being a

"Vatican puppet" or a pre-Vatican II reactionary. But keep in mind what Christ has said:

> If you find that the world hates you know that it has hated me before you. If you belonged to the world it would love you as its own; the reason it hates you is that you do not belong to the world. ...

> ... whoever acknowledges me before men — the Son of man will acknowledge him before the angels of God. But the man who has disowned me in the presence of men will be disowned in the presence of the angels of God.

FOOTNOTES

[1] "First Draft — Bishops' Pastoral Letter. Catholic Social Teaching and the U. S. Economy," *Origins,* Vol. 14: No. 22/23, November 15, 1984, p. 345. Hereinafter referred to as "Bishops' Pastoral Letter and the Economy."

[2] **Ibid.**, pp. 345-346. The extensive discussion of the Old Testament vision of economic life in the letter explains perhaps the overstressing of justice and the narrowing of the community in the exaltation of the "chosen people" — those who reside in a democracy.

[3] **Ibid.**, p. 346.

[4] John Paul II, "On Human Work," U. S. Catholic Conference, Washington, D. C., 1981.

[5] **Ibid.**, p. 53.

[6] "Bishops' Pastoral Letter and the Economy," p. 351.

[7] **Ibid.**

[8] **Ibid.**

[9] **Ibid.**, p. 352.

[10] **Ibid.**, p. 351.

[11] **Ibid.**, p. 355.

[12] **Ibid.**

[13] **Ibid.**, p. 357.

[14] **Ibid.**

[16] **Ibid.**, p. 363.

[17] **Ibid.**, p. 369.

[18] **Ibid.**, p. 367.

[19] **Ibid.**, p. 372.

[20] **Ibid.**, p. 375.

[21] "The Challenge of Peace: God's Promise and Our Response. A Pastoral Letter on War and Peace," National Conference of Catholic Bishops, May 3, 1983.

[22] See pp. 19, 25, 29, 78-79, 98.

[23] "Bishops' Pastoral Letter and the Economy," p. 367.

[24] Eugene Kennedy, "Coming of Age in America," *Notre Dame Magazine,* Winter 1984/85, Vol. 13, No. 5, pp. 17-18. This essay describes an attitude which is especially helpful in understanding the support for Mario Cuomo. On page 18, it is said that "Mario Cuomo stands for all the men and women of his generation who stepped out of the longing dream of their immigrant forebears. He symbolizes in himself the successful outcome of a century of immigrant sacrifice for Catholic education. His generation of Catholics was transformed by the will and generosity of their parents and grandparents into first-class, fully privileged Americans participating in the work and life of the nation on an equal footing. These Catholics are now found everywhere in the American culture. . . . They are exactly what their Catholic educators hoped they would become: . . . ." Catholic laymen like Mario Cuomo: "are crucial source[s] of revelation" for "the contemporary Church."

Comment on the Bishops' Pastoral Letter

by

Philip F. Lawler

We all owe Regis Factor a deep debt of gratitude, not only for his fine paper, but also for pointing out to us the possibility that the thought of Mario Cuomo constitutes revelation. I look forward to the working of the historical-critical method on Cuomo's work. Still, I must caution against too deep a commitment to the validity of Governor Cuomo's revelation. As you may know already, some leading analysts believe that Mario Cuomo was never elected Governor of New York. The popular belief in that myth (these experts continue) reflects the decision of the *New York Times* to *speak of* Cuomo as "Governor" in order to better explain the affective power of the "Cuomo experience."

My own reflections on the first draft of the bishops' pastoral letter are not so much scholarly as practical. During the past three years, I have been involved as an active participant in the debates surrounding the pastoral letter and the bishops' previous statements on nuclear weapons.

Of all the practical lessons I have learned during these debates, the most important is this: when the bishops begin work on a pastoral letter, the discussion inevitably takes place on two largely unrelated planes. The first plane involves the actual wording of the bishops' letter and the theological underpinning for their arguments. The second involves the public *perception* of what the bishops have said — a perception which may or may not match the actual content of the pastoral letter.

Scholars who study the bishops' pastoral letters would do well to remember this two-level approach to the debate. Such scholars may read every paragraph of the pastoral letter carefully and measure the bishops' efforts against the context of a century's tradition of Catholic social teachings. But the overwhelming majority of Catholics (and non-Catholics, of course) will not read the pastoral letter carefully, if they read it at all. Nor are they acquainted with Catholic social teachings. On the contrary, the overwhelming majority will learn about the pastoral letter through news reports in the secular media and judge it against the other headlines of the day's political battles.

So it is that, in my own experience, I have found that most audiences see the bishops' letters as *solely* political documents. Most audiences two years ago saw the "peace pastoral" as simply an endorsement of the nuclear freeze. Most audiences today see the first draft of the economics pastoral as simply an attack on the policies of the Reagan administration. In fact, many audiences are genuinely surprised to learn that the bishops have offered anything *more* than an indictment of Reaganomics. The arguments that most intrigue scholars — arguments about the just-war tradition and pacifism on the one hand, subsidiarity and social justice on the other — are almost completely irrelevant to the popular understanding of the bishops' documents.

However, scholars cannot be content with the realization that the argument is being conducted on two levels. The next logical step is to discover which of the two parallel arguments is, ultimately, more important. Particularly in this case, if the issues were framed properly, there can be no doubt that the more important debate would revolve around the actual content of the bishops' message, rather than the accompanying political posturing. But, at least in the first draft, the issues are not framed properly.

Our bishops are facing an enormous opportunity to advance the social teachings of the Catholic Church. The Church has always viewed capitalism with considerable skepticism, and understandably so. Capitalism, in and of itself, provides no moral compass to guide human actions toward the common good. However, as an instrument of economic development, capitalism has been enormously successful, and this success cannot be taken lightly by anyone who cares for the temporal welfare of the people. If they applied traditional Catholic social teachings to the particular experiences of American society, our bishops might find ways to adapt capitalism, increasing its moral sensitivity without compromising its practical utility.

To accomplish the task of their pastoral letter, the bishops must act as advocates of two different traditions. Many Americans complain that the Church does not understand the U. S. economic system. Many Catholics, on the other hand, complain that Americans do not understand Catholic social teachings. Personally, I think both complaints are largely accurate. It remains for the bishops, acting as intermediaries between the two traditions, to open the lines of communication.

In fact, the bishops' first draft ignores that challenge. Many analysts have criticized the draft for its failure to portray the American economy accurately, and Dr. Dechert will add his voice to those protests. Let me, therefore, address the question of how well the draft captures the tradition of Catholic social thought.

That question can be answered fairly directly. The draft virtually ignores the most important thematic elements of Catholic social thought. Consider, for instance, the draft's treatment of the following themes:

— **Subsidiarity.** Probably the single most important element in the Catholic tradition of social analysis, the principle of subsidiarity weighs heavily against centralized decision-making. The draft pays lip service to subsidiarity, it is true, but the practical recommendations embodied in the draft — and the economic analysis underlying those recommendations — are thoroughly oriented toward central government solutions for economic problems.

— **The Common Good.** What is the standard against which we measure a society's success? How can we know whether the nation's resources are being employed productively (i.e., to the benfit of the whole society)? The draft makes no effort to explain the Catholic notion of the common good. Nor does it offer any explanation of what Pope John Paul means when he refers (as he so frequently does) to the need for "socialization" of economic functions. Too often, American readers are left to assume that "socialization" is more or less synonymous with "nationalization," and thus that the Pope favors socialism.

— **Family Wages.** Today, American society celebrates the "working mother," who leaves her young children in a child-care center while she pursues her career. The bishops take note of this problem, but the solutions proposed in the first draft center around the need for better (government subsidized) child care. Traditionally, the Church has taught that a just wage should allow a man to support his family, so that his wife does not have to work. That message might not be popular with an American audience today. But it is, indisputably, an important aspect of Catholic social teaching.

— **Poverty.** The first draft makes no distinction between physical and spiritual poverty, so that someone reading that draft could be forgiven for thinking that the ecclesiastical vow of poverty is a device whereby the quintessential American *bourgeois* can transform himself into a member of the oppressed class — without sacrificing any of his creature comforts. Surely there is a crucial distinction between spiritual poverty, which is good, and physical poverty, which is a tragedy. And surely our society would be immeasurably enriched if more wealthy people acquired the virtue of spiritual poverty.

These glaring omissions constitute the most serious defects in the bishops' first draft since they represent the bishops' (or, rather, the drafting committee's) failure to advance the fundamental principles of Catholic social teaching. But there are some real difficulties with what the draft *does* say, as well.

Consider, for instance, the draft's complaint that our society "violates the minimum standards of distributive justice." By any of the normal statistical indices, American society does a better job of distributing wealth than most other societies past and present. Do *all* societies violate these minimum standards? In our own society, the distribution of wealth has changed significantly in recent years. Are we to conclude, then, that America has been in violation of these "minimum standards" for some time? And if so, why have the bishops never previously mentioned this fact?

Or consider the draft's insistence that unemployment should be cut down to a rate of no more than 4 percent. The draft admits that most reputable economists agree that a 4 percent unemployment rate has become impossible to maintain under contemporary economic conditions. Nevertheless, the draft holds that figure up — not as an ideal but as a moral imperative. Nowhere does the draft explain how the 4 percent figure was reached. Why not 5 percent? Or 3 percent? If the bishops intend to judge economic morality against a statistical measure, surely they must explain how that statistical measure has been created.

These are only two of the most obvious analytical weaknesses in the draft pastoral letter. Similar problems abound. But, as I mentioned at the outset, my particular concern in these comments is the draft's failure to make the positive case for Catholic social teaching.

Somehow, instead of promoting the Church's distinctive vision for our society, the bishops' first draft has managed to place the Church on the defensive. Since the release of the first draft and particularly during the Holy Father's visit to Latin America, newspaper editorials have wondered aloud why the Church is speaking out about the problem of world poverty. After all, the editorialists reason, the Church *aggravates* the problem of poverty, by refusing to allow population control through artificial contraception.

If the bishops were to take an aggressive posture in their discussion of economics, they could address that criticism head-on. The editorialists, alas, are reflecting an idea that has a great deal of popular support in today's America — the idea that people are the *cause* of poverty, rather than the potential cure. Very few voices today are fighting against that misguided idea. Again, the American bishops may be missing a dramatic opportunity.

If they are not representing the best traditions of Catholic thought, what are the bishops seeking to accomplish in this pastoral letter? Is their ultimate objective to influence the public debate on issues surrounding the political economy? Is the popular perception — that the bishops are engaged in a purely political task — functionally accurate? If that is the case, then the bishops are subverting their own moral authority.

The first draft of the economics pastoral, like the late drafts of the preceding pastoral letter on nuclear weaponry, emphasizes that the bishops speak with different levels of moral authority. When they affirm the doctrinal stance of the Church, they speak with the full authority of their charism. But when they make practical judgments on prudential political considerations, laymen may reasonably disagree. That distinction (which, not coincidentally, was emphasized at the request of the Vatican) is a sound one.

Still, to emphasize that distinction is to run a companion risk. Most casual readers of the bishops' pastoral letters will understand that the bishops' judgments are debatable. But will they understand that not *all* hierarchical decisions are debatable? To state the question differently, can the bishops reasonably expect the laity to understand the nature of their authority, as well as its limitations?

Few Catholics would doubt that the bishops' economic analysis is fallible. Indeed, the real danger in the bishops' enterprise is the possibility that ordinarily faithful Catholics will begin assuming that the bishops' statements are *never* definitive — that the individual has the option to accept or reject *any* aspect of Catholic doctrine. At the outset of this first draft and at the outset of the "peace pastoral," the bishops, in effect, confess that their work is open to question. Can there be any surer way for the bishops to undermine their own teaching authority?

Maritain and
Natural Rights Revisited

by

Ralph McInerny

Readers of Alasdair MacIntyre's **After Virtue** will have been struck by an apparent inconsistency. He says that Maritain is someone from whom he has learned much, presumably on the subjects discussed in the book. Yet one of the key arguments of his book is that natural rights are fictions.

The opposition can be sharpened. It is well known that Jacques Maritain regarded the UN universal declaration on human rights as a landmark. His attitude toward the United Nations reflects the optimism and enthusiasm of the first years of that organization. In the speech he gave to the second international conference on UNESCO in Mexico City *(La Voie de la Paix,* Librairie Francaise, Mexico City, 1947), Maritain gave expression to views further developed in **Man and the State** in 1951. By contrast, this is what MacIntyre has to say:

> In the United Nations declaration on human rights of 1949 what has since become the normal UN practice of not giving good reasons for *any* assertions whatsoever is followed with great rigour. And the latest defender of such rights, Ronald Dworkin **(Taking Rights Seriously,** 1976) concedes that the existence of such rights cannot be demonstrated, but remarks on this point simply that it does not follow from the fact that a statement cannot be demonstrated that it is not true ... Natural and human rights then are fictions — just as is utility — but fictions with highly specific properties. (p. 67)

My aim in this paper is to look at Maritain's remarks on human or natural rights from our end-of-the-century viewpoint to see how precisely he admitted the doctrine of natural rights into his political philosophy and to see whether he has provided defenses against the kind of criticism MacIntyre has developed.

Nothing comes easier to a Thomist than to notice that much has been lost in ethical and political theory in recent centuries that is essential to the fashioning of a doctrine of rights. When Maritain called for an end of Machiavellianism, he insisted that classical and medieval moral and political thought are meant to apply to men as they are: fallen men, men of flesh and blood. To dismiss such thought as the idle idealizations of the underemployed is a libel against them. As practical philosophy, classical and medieval thought was meant to be action-guiding. *Realpolitik,* on the other hand, cannot be described as taking men as they are and trying to lead them to the good. Rather, it is a matter of accepting evils and trying to turn them to the selfish interests of individuals and groups.

Thomistic moral and political philosophy addresses man in his totality — what he is, in the sense of his failures, faults, and sinfulness; and what he can and ought to be, in terms of the teleology of his nature, his role in creation.

Prima facie, one would expect a Thomist like Maritain to be in profound sympathy with MacIntyre, to agree with him about the failure of the Enlightenment Project, and to insist that modern theory is so denatured as to have no basis for the erection of a doctrine of rights. Surely, it would be odd in the extreme to cast Maritain in the role of defender of the Enlightenment, or defender of any of MacIntyre's chief targets. Students of Jacques Maritain will think immediately of **Moral Philosophy: An Historical and Critical Survey of the Great Systems** as counter evidence. Nonetheless, Maritain defends the doctrine of natural rights, with specific reference to the UN declaration, and I want to review his teaching here. It will — to no one's surprise — turn out to be a good deal more complicated than the simplistic opposition my proem suggests.

Les Droits de l'homme et la loi naturelle, published in 1941 (cf. **Oeuvres,** ed. Bars, vol 2, pp. 165-228) provides a good beginning for us. After a moving passage in which he argues that the currents of liberty and fraternity opened by the Gospels, the virtues of justice and friendships sanctioned by them, their emphasis on the human person, and authority's ultimate answerability to God, provide the internal energy for civilization to reach its fulfillment, Maritain says this:

> Ceux qui ne croient pas en Dieu ou qui ne professent pas le christianisme, si cependant ils croient a la dignite de la personne humaine, a la justice, a la liberte, a l'amour du prochain, peuvent cooperer eux aussi a la realisation d'une telle conception de la societe, et cooperer au bien commun, alors meme qu'ils ne savent pas remonter jusqu'aux premiers principes de leurs convictions pratiques, ou cherchent a fonder celles-ci sur des principes deficients.   (p. 177)

Maritain has written this as a commentary on the fourth of the four characteristics he feels essential to a society of free men: that it be personalist, communitarian, pluralist, and theist or Christian. He is not laying out a plan for a theocracy or for a government that could only be realized by believing Christians. He is speaking of the only kind of society befitting free human beings. Such a society must be theist, even Christian, in the sense that there is recognized in it the dignity of the human person, justice, liberty, and love of neighbor, *on whatever basis these be held.*

The basis may not be the only adequate and sufficient one — the derivation of creation, man included, from God — but may either be a basis short of that, yet dependent on it, or — and this is what is extraordinary — may even be deficient principles.

Such critiques of modernity as MacIntyre's argue from the deficiency of the principle from which rights are derived to the conclusion that the resultant rights are fictions, a criticism which reaches its apotheosis when confronted with the blithe admission that natural rights cannot be proved at all. Anyone who has been impressed by the opening sweep of chapters of **After Virtue** may fear that, by contrast, Maritain's assumption that universal consent to the four characteristics of society can be gained is hopelessly naive. What would be gained besides a willingness to mouth mere words? Can a theory antithetical to Maritain's own theism ground natural rights? It is to Chapter IV of **Man and the State** that we must turn for a discussion of these fundamental issues.

The first section of that chapter bears the ringing assertion: *Men mutually opposed in their theoretical conceptions can come to a merely practical agreement regarding a list of human rights.* This section opens with the remark that we nowadays have come to a fuller realization of a number of practical truths about human life, and it is this alleged progress in realization that has gone hand in hand with a divergence in theoretical conceptions (which depend on ideological allegiance, philosophical and religious traditions, cultural backgrounds, and historical experiences). He takes the Universal Declaration of 1948 to be proof that men can, with whatever difficulty, achieve a common formulation of such practical conclusions which are "the various rights possessed by man in his personal and social existence" (p. 76). Maritain continues:

> Yet it would be quite futile to look for a common rational justification of these practical conclusions and these rights. If we did so we would run the risk of imposing arbitrary dogmatism or of being stopped short by irreconcilable differences. The question raised at this point is that of the practical agreement among men who are theoretically opposed to one another. **(Ibid.)**

Although indispensable, he writes, rational justifications are powerless to create agreement among men. They are indispensable because everyone believes instinctively in the truth and wishes to give consent only to what is true and rationally valid. The powerlessness of theoretical justifications to create agreement is attributed to their plurality and their backgrounds out of which the plurality of justifications arise.

Maritain recognizes that he is holding a paradoxical position. Let us take a moment to stress its difficulties. There are certain practical judgments about what should be done, on which all men can agree despite the fact that they have radically different ways of justifying those judgments. A. MacIntyre suggests that such radical diversity affects the very meanings of the judgments and thus makes agreement merely verbal. Unfortunately, Maritain gives no examples here, and I will not provide one, lest it skew the discussion. He notices that the UN Rights of Man Declaration commanded agreement from the various signatories *provided we are not asked why.* "With the 'why,' the dispute begins" (p. 77).

At this point, Maritain quotes from his UNESCO address, cited earlier:

> How is an agreement conceivable among men assembled for the purpose of jointly accomplishing a task dealing with the future of the mind, who come from the four corners of the earth and who belong not only to different spiritual families but to antagonistic schools of thought? Since the aim of UNESCO is a practical aim, agreement among its members can be spontaneously achieved, not on common speculative notions, but on common practical notions; not on the affirmation of the same conception of the world, man, and knowledge, but on the affirmation of the same set of convictions concerning action. This is doubtless very little; it is the last refuge of intellectual agreement among men. It is, however, enough to undertake a great work; and it would mean a great deal to become aware of this body of common practical convictions.   (77-78)

Men do not share a common speculative ideology or common explanatory principles, but "... the basic *practical* ideology and the basic principles of *action* implicitly recognized today, ... constitute *grosso modo* a sort of common residue, a sort of unwritten common law" (78).

Now this sounds extremely strange. It may seem to do little more than recall those halcyon postwar days when it was possible to look upon the United Nations with hope. But the decades since have taught us that the language of rights has put a weapon into the hands of those for whom words have meanings diametrically opposed to those we understand. The Soviet Union is a signatory of the Universal Declaration, and its understanding of human rights is opposed to our own not simply on the level of theoretical ideology and explanatory principles, but precisely in the practical order. Maritain's last refuge of intellectual agreement seems to be the last refuge of scoundrels:

> To understand that [common practical agreement] it is sufficient to distinguish properly between a rational justification, inseparable from the spiritual dynamism of a philosophical doctrine or religious faith, and the practical conclusions which, separately justified for each, are, for all, analogically common principles of action. I am fully convinced that my way of justifying the belief in the rights of man and the ideal of freedom, equality, and fraternity is the only one which is solidly based on truth. That does not prevent me from agreeing on these practical tenets with those who are convinced that their way of justifying them, entirely different from mine or even opposed to mine in its theoretical dynamism, is likewise the only one that is based on truth. (p. 78)

But the problem is: what will freedom, equality and fraternity mean, and mean practically? Maritain sees the agreement that produced the Universal Declaration as pragmatic, not theoretical, and feels that nothing "prevents the attainment of formulations which would indicate notable progress in the process of world unification" (79).

This makes sad reading today. The pragmatic agreement has been a snare and a delusion, and it would seem naive to deny it. To the degree that Maritain's teaching here is linked to the fact of the UN, it seems to have been pretty well weakened, if not completely refuted by history. That is, there has been a pragmatic disproof.

Does this mean that, since MacIntyre is surely right about the Universal Declaration and Maritain is surely wrong, that we must agree with the former that the notion of common human rights is simply a fiction? Clearly not. The Church speaks to us again and again in terms of the rights of all human persons and regards these rights as natural; that is, while the reminder comes to us in Church documents, while our conviction about such rights shares in the certainty of our divine faith, *what* we are being reminded of or *what* we are certain of are rights that can be naturally recognized. Let us go further: *they are natural rights that are actually recognized by men.*

What I want to do in the remainder of this paper is to develop a version of Maritain's linking of natural rights to natural law which enables us to see the defensibility of his teaching on these matters.

Jacques Maritain makes it quite clear in **Man and the State** what the theoretical foundation of the doctrine of natural rights is. It is quite simply the natural law, properly understood (p. 80). There may be many competitive theoretical or ideological statements put forward in justification of natural rights, but, for Maritain, only one of them is the true one. Furthermore, if it is true, it will provide an explanation of how there can be, despite the plurality of theoretical justifications, an agreement in the practical order.

In putting forward a sketch of natural law, Maritain makes his famous distinction between the first element of natural law, which is ontological, and the second, which is gnosiological. Not a very promising distinction, you might think, since, if law is as such *aliquid rationis*, it would seem always to be gnosiological and never merely ontological.

By the ontological element of natural law, Maritain means man's nature, in virtue of which he possesses ends which necessarily correspond to his essential constitution and which are the same for all. Every natural and artificial thing has a nature in the relevant sense, but man is endowed with intelligence and determines his own ends, and he must put himself in tune with the ends necessarily demanded by his nature. Maritain writes:

> This means that there is, by the very virtue of human nature, an order or a disposition which human reason can discover and according to which the human will must act in order to attune itself to the essential and necessary ends of the human being. The unwritten law, or natural law, is nothing more than that. (p. 86)

But what precisely is the ontological element of natural law? He answers: "... the *normality of functioning* which is grounded on the essence of that being: man" (p. 87-8). The second element of natural law, the gnosiological, is "natural law *as known,* and, thus, as measuring in actual fact human practical reason, which is the measure of human acts" (p. 89). The only practical knowledge all men have naturally and infallibly in common as a self-evident principle, intellectually perceived by virtue of the concepts involved, is that we must do good and avoid evil. But this is not so much natural law as its principle or preamble. "Natural law," Maritain writes, "... is the ensemble of things to do and not to do which follow therefrom in *necessary* fashion" (p. 90). Every sort of error and deviation is possible in the determination of these things.

Another distinctive note of Maritain's understanding of natural law is the contention that it is an instance of knowledge through inclination (p. 91).

It is tempting to want to worry over the niceties and details of even so swift a presentation of the doctrine of natural law as we find in Chapter IV of **Man and the State.** On another occasion I might succumb to that temptation, but before such an audience as this it would be presumptuous to do. I shall end my paper with an attempt to express, a la Maritain, who, of course, develops his own views a la St. Thomas Aquinas, the resolution of the seeming paradox of his position.

What again is the paradox, not to say the seemingly insuperable difficulty, of what Maritain so often says in connection with such documents as the Universal Charter?

On the one hand, there is the fact that a great many signatories have surprisingly agreed to the declaration. On the other hand, there is the fact that they would put forward differing and incompatible justifications which may vary from inadequacy to outright untruth. But is it possible to separate the understanding of the rights, and the sense of the agreement, from the explanations and justifications that are given of them?

Natural law precepts beyond do good and avoid evil, even though they express ways of acting necessarily connected with the ends of human nature are formulated only with difficulty, with much veering and careening and intermittent error. In what sense of 'same' could the same precepts be formulated on the basis of radically different theoretical assumptions?

Maritain would say that what we are talking about is the gnosiological natural law, but surely any declaration of rights would pertain to the gnosiological, and it is here that differences are rife. The only hope for Maritain's position would seem to be this: *the verbal agreement on a list of rights which are justified theoretically in many and incompatible ways is founded, not on those different justifications, but rather on what he calls the ontological natural law.*

This means, I take it, that even inadequate and false justifications have embedded in them an implicit recognition of the true ends of human nature and, thus, of the true basis for practical precepts.

As a theory, natural law may be one theory among others. But if it is a sound theory, there must be certain truths about the practical order that no man can fail to know. Nonetheless, men think that ways of action incompatible with precepts of natural law are true. Despite this, there is at bottom a common implicit recognition of man's true good.

Now this does not mean that when someone thinks that the direct killing of the innocent is sometimes justified, he or she *really* thinks the exact opposite. What it does mean is that such a person already knows that which will show his or her judgment to be wrong. The preamble and principle of natural law are already implicitly known by every human agent. The means of refuting our erroneous judgments are already possessed by us and, indeed, latent in the process whereby we make the erroneous judgments. This means the that verbal acceptance of the rights of man, while it may in a given case profess to be based on grounds that are false, can be grounded on bases already implicitly known by the one making the erroneous judgment.

If I judge that the direct killing of the innocent is sometimes permitted, I am judging that such an action will be fulfilling and perfective of the kind of agent I am. The fundamental criterion of my judgments is the human good, what is perfective of the kind of agent I am.

In the example, I have mistakenly taken a certain kind of action to be conducive to that good or an articulation of it. If then, I can be made to see that actions of this type are always and everywhere inimical to the human good, destructive of it, *I already have a basis for changing my mind*. Changing my ways is a different and more difficult matter, but until and unless I come to see that my practical judgment is actually inimical to the good I had thought it conducive to, existential change cannot occur.

Whether or not this is equivalent to Maritain's distinction between the ontological and gnosiological elements of natural law, it is similar to it. My distinction is perhaps better described as one between implicit and explicit knowledge of natural law. But is my distinction sufficient to explain the agreement among signatories or wildly different outlooks on a list of human rights? I don't think so. I am not sure that Maritain has succeeded in giving an explanation of that agreement either — that is, succeeded in showing that it is indeed an agreement that goes beyond mere words which have radically different meanings for different signatories.

An agreement which must accomodate the kind of ideological cleavage between the West and the East seems necessarily empty. The history of the United Nations since Maritain wrote **Man and the State** cannot be ignored. Decades of experience on the part of truce teams, arms talks teams, and human rights commissions, cannot be ignored.

An agreement that is not one of substance, assuring the same meaning of the same words and the same scheme of justification, is no agreement at all. There is no shortcut to such agreement. The Universal Declaration resides, as MacIntyre suggested, on a fiction.

Nonetheless, there is embedded in the very disagreements the possibility of agreement. Call it the ontological natural law, call it the implicit knowledge of natural law precepts which is compatible with explicit knowledge at partial variance with them; whatever, human persons can come to agreement on human nature and human rights but only on the basis of the truth.

The Catholic has a powerful reminder of the reality of human rights in innumerable documents of the Ordinary Magisterium and the declarations of Vatican II. One need not be a believer to recognize those rights, however practically necessary it is for fallen man to have that supernatural setting for natural knowledge. But the non-believer must understand the true basis for those rights, or it is not human rights he is recognizing.

Just as Jacques Maritain held that a true understanding of natural law is the only adequate justification of human rights, so the Church reminds us that the common human supernatural destiny is the chief basis for the value of the human person. Isn't that what Maritain was saying in explaining the fourth characteristic of a society befitting free men?

Public Morality in Liberal Democracy: "E Pluribus Duo"

by

John A. Gueguen

My task here is to explain in twenty minutes why there is fundamental disagreement in our country over right and wrong.[1] It has always been puzzling to me why Americans do not or cannot agree that social evils like divorce, artificial contraception, abortion, homosexuality, and pornography are in fact evil and ought therefore to be condemned and extirpated.

One could attribute the disagreement, I suppose, to orneriness or to the all-too-human face-saving device of rationalization. We are all good at that. But even people who seriously and sincerely sit down to reason out these matters of public morality seem to read the moral nature of man the hence the moral law of God differently. Why?

My immediate perception is that there is nothing wrong with human nature (given the metaphysical limitations of participated beings) nor with the moral law (given the perfection of its Author). In the abstract, man is all that he *can* be, and God is all that He *is*. The problem, I conclude, must therefore lie elsewhere. Could it be in the way Americans have been taught their morality — at home, in church, at school, and in a public forum that is itself divided on all these issues?

Many scholars, concerned over increasing signs of moral decay, have urged a recurrence to our national origins — whether as democratic society or as republican regime.[2] They assure us that our "tradition" holds the potential for recovery of a moral consensus which is in agreement with human nature and the moral law. Some even argue that the genius of the American Founding and Judeo-Christian ethics harmonize in principle. It is often alleged that America is a Christian nation.

My studies of American political thought, of the "tradition" to which these scholars appeal, lead me to a different conclusion. I find that such a harmony is largely, if not entirely, illusory.

Three years ago in *Communio*, my good friend, Walter Nicgorski of Notre Dame, conducted a discussion of "Democracy and Moral-Religious Neutrality: American and Catholic Perspectives."[3] I wish to see if I can extend that discussion here. While he did distinguish between the principles of the American regime and Catholic principles of morality, Dr. Nicgorski was looking for signs of convergence between them. If my persuasion is correct — that no single "tradition" exists in our country which could be called both American and Christian — then any convergence would at best be accidental.

I wish to suggest in these remarks that America has witnessed two foundings, that two traditions grow out of these foundings, and that they are irreconcilable in essentials (that is, in their premises about man's nature and God's law). In developing this argument, I want to show that the recent public debate over morality and policy can help to elucidate the truth about moral life and its connection with political life. When the 1984 campaign gave these topics more prominence than the media usually permit, many people were mortified at what they regarded an unseemly and even threatening exposure of matters they thought should remain private. But since the correctness or incorrectness of moral norms is bound to affect the good or ill fortunes of society, I believe that it is urgent for us to continue and extend that public discussion — without, I hope, its rancor and obfuscation.

More than fifty years ago Jacques Maritain wrote: "Certain essential principles seem to have been lost sight of by many people, and it is of the first importance that they be recalled." He set about in **The Things That Are Not Caesar's** to "tell the truth as it appears to me, without regard for any other consideration." [4] It is in that spirit that I proceed.

Maritain insisted that democracies cannot subsist without a Christian orientation, especially in an era when both have their backs against the wall. *He* was mortified, he said in **Christianity and Democracy**, because the modern democracies were "repudiating" the Gospel in the name of human liberty, while at the same time "motivating forces in the Christian social strata" were combatting democratic aspirations.[5]

Is this, perhaps, because of a fundamental discontinuity between the two, or is it due to circumstances that have occurred over the 300 years of our national existence?

To some extent the relationship between Judeo-Christian ethics and the morality implicit in modern liberal democracy contains the seeds of tensions and disagreements lately aired in our country, thus making it difficult to resolve them to the satisfaction of the one or of the other. This situation is complicated by historical developments peculiar to America, which seem to have converted the tension into an antithesis which must continue to trouble and divide the nation until one side succeeds in driving the other from the field.

In one of his great ironic utterances about Christianity and democracy, G. K. Chesterton remarked: "Christianity says that anyone can be a saint if he chooses; democracy says that anyone can be a citizen if he chooses." [6] This is ironic, I think, because Christianity makes the choosing difficult for the would-be citizen, and democracy makes the choosing difficult for the would-be saint. Why is this? The same Chesterton observed of Christianity that, even when it is watered down, it is still "hot enough to boil modern society to rags." [7] And when he observed in America that our corporate ideal is citizenship in a multinational society,[8] he implied that it is an ideal cold and deliberate enough to freeze aspirations to practice the Christian virtues heroically — the minimum condition for sainthood.

If Christian morality and liberal democracy are not easy companions and, in some sense, even threats to one another, what does this imply for our historical attempts to construct a society which is both Christian and democratic? Further, what do those attempts contribute to the moral disorders which, according to many reports, are propelling our society along toward dissolution?

In speaking of Christian morality, I do not wish to obscure the distinction between morality and religion. Certainly morality has a natural basis that makes its principles accessible to every thinking person. Morality is much broader than religion in that it includes principles drawn from sources other than those contained in a supernatural revelation. Nevertheless, morality can be and, in the case of Judeo-Christianity, has been brought within religion and made a part of it. For while the author of the first great treatise on ethics was not concerned with religion, the Author of the definitive sourcebook on religion surely was concerned with moral acts and had plenty to say about them. If Aristotle is therefore neutral on religion, the Bible is surely not neutral on morality.

Now America has been, since its origins, a land of religious plurality. If every religion teaches morality, and if different expressions or interpretations of religion teach different things, then religious plurality must imply moral plurality. Different conclusions must arise from conflicting premises. Moreover, every moral teaching has political implications, just as every political theory contains moral implications. Consequently, students of American history are reminded in every textbook that "religion" has had a great influence on public life, a formative influence on our civic culture. But these texts seldom, if ever, go on to specify *which* religion they mean, nor do they differentiate between the two opposed religious traditions which I want now to discuss — two spirits, as it were, intent upon building two cities.

I must confess that, after many years of teaching American political thought, it has been a quite recent discovery that there have been these *two* traditions of political thought in America: the one everyone apparently understands by it (which is really Protestant and anthropocentric), and one which none of the commentators seem to be conscious of (which is Catholic and theocentric).

Here I have time to trace only the merest outline of the twin development of these two spirits since the days when Americans became conscious of themselves as distinct from their European forebears.

The Protestant ethic proceeds from the Puritan settlement in the Northeast through the period of the Constitutional founding and 19th-century Transcendentalism into the Pragmatism which has dominated our century. From the beginning, this tradition has tended to adapt Christian morality to the needs of civil society, as defined by its human builders, and to make moral principles serve republican interests.

The Catholic ethic proceeds from the Franciscan settlement in the Southwest through the period of the establishment of a church hierarchy at the time of national independence into the 19th century, when the first systematic efforts were made to bring it to consciousness as a different tradition. With the exception of Father John Courtney Murray,[9] these efforts seem to have been submerged in our century by a desire to accomodate the Catholic minority to the Protestant majority. Or spokesmen have not appeared who are well enough formed in the Catholic tradition or sufficiently accomplished as writers to promote it effectively. From the beginning, the Catholic ethic tended to adapt secular situations to the promotion of a truth about man by making those situations serve the moral imperatives found in the Gospel.

The Protestant version of American public morality presumes the anthropocentrism of the social contract theory and reads it into democratic theory. It makes the individual autonomous and self-directing. It accepts God's law only to the extent that human objectives are well served. Human imperfections are excused or overlooked; moral truth is considered a matter of private opinion; freedom is made a subjective prerogative; politics is given the task of transforming the earth. It is a short step from there to "liberation theology."

In the recent debates, one can find a fundamental agreement within the Protestant tradition between the old Left and the New Right that the Kingdom of God is (or must be made) *in* America, that it is a "dynamic process" (the words are H. Richard Niebuhr's) in quest of social liberation through the manipulation of political institutions, and not a creed, a discipline that transcends all nations as it strives to liberate all persons from their own infirmities before they can undertake to relieve man's estate.[10]

Thus the Catholic version of American public morality is the exact reverse of the one that now dominates our country. Founded on acceptance of the social nature of man, it expresses a theocentric ethic which subordinates every human objective to God's work of Redemption. Without diminishing the personal responsibility of every man for his own salvation, individual autonomy gives way to an ecclesial community whose assistance is essential in making our way to heaven. God's law makes demands for sacrifice, conversion, a constant struggle to improve one's life and to help others improve. Moral truth is a matter of fact, discoverable by reason and clarified by revelation. Free action is informed by objective norms. The glory of politics is to have no human glory but to provide an orderly passage through this radically imperfect and precarious world. There is no better recent summary of this doctrine than in the documents of Vatican II, especially the Constitution on the Church in the Modern World.

Compare the self-conscious and sombre legalism of Winthrop's Boston with the almost carefree political minimalism of Serra's California missions.[11] Or compare the defensiveness of James Madison's federal republican principle with the unitary principle of hereditary authority which grounded John Carroll's aggressive apostolate.[12] Or compare the individualistic musings of Emerson with the communitarian conscience of Brownson in the period of our great national trauma.[13] Whichever comparison you choose to develop, the contrast is striking and, I think, most instructive.

Is the moral purpose of America to bring God's laws into conformity with the sovereign people, or is it to bring the people into conformity with God's sovereign laws? Is the moral purpose of America to train people in virtue because of its usefulness to civil order, or is it to train civil institutions so that they will promote individual virtue? Should moral norms be bent to accomodate civil exigencies (such as an alleged pressure of population upon resources), or should civil norms be bent to accomodate moral exigencies (such as the innocence of children)? Public discourse is divided because there is precedent in America for both sides of each question.

An understanding of the relation between public morality and liberal democracy in the American context will continue to elude us, I believe, until we become more aware of the two traditions, and especially of the one which our studies, even in Catholic universities, have so much neglected. Unless its own roots, its own founding, and its own development are brought to full consciousness, we shall continue to be puzzled by the controversies over morality and policy that swirl over the landscape like a fog.

More regrettably, we shall continue to be scandalized by prominent Catholics who accept the Protestant tradition, and even defend and further it, because they are unaware or confused about their own tradition. We shall continue to be embarrassed, without knowing quite what to do about it, by colleagues of ours who are more intent upon telling the magisterial Teacher of the Catholic ethic what America is all about [14] than on telling Americans about the magisterial Teacher.

If my assessment of the underlying reason for a lack of moral consensus in our nation is correct, then the rhetoric about a struggle for its soul is hardly an exaggeration. But this struggle need not evoke fear or regret. During the late presidential campaign, the bishops of New England (no longer Puritan but now predominantly Catholic New England) said: "The moment in which we find ourselves, while it may be discomforting for some, appears to us a splendid opportunity for clarifying some fundamental principles" concerning the interaction of morality and policy.[15] We cannot clarify that interaction, however, as it seems to me, until we have understood the opposed traditions within the moral component.

In the latest critique of the American "civil religion," an "artifact of the secularizing process," as he calls it, Professor George Armstrong Kelly proclaims the death of the Protestant era in America, its denominations having failed to exercise an authority capable of stemming the nation's slide into neopaganism.[16] If his perception is correct, we have a new reason to entertain Maritain's vision of an America full of potential for a new Christian civilization, a society of citizen-saints. In his **Reflections on America** he could already see the unacceptable moral consequences of a civil religion which allows God's law to be "temporalized."[17]

An exciting time of realignment lies ahead, I believe, as we enter what may come to be the Catholic era in America — or better, the Catholic Reformation of American moral and political life. We need not fear (though we do lament) the loss of many Catholic leaders whose minds and lives have been Protestantized, for there are increasing indications that the minds and lives of many Protestant leaders have been Catholicized.

With Richard John Neuhaus, then, we can agree that the present confusion "can turn out to be a watershed moment in American political and cultural life."[18] While its detailed elaboration cannot be foreseen, Father George Rutler has made one condition for the successful navigation of this watershed very clear: "The conscience of the public Catholic needs to embrace the Catholic conception of morality," and not as a cold formula "extrinsically imposed, but as intrinsic to the human condition." [19] This can come to pass only if Catholic scholars do the hard work that is needed to recover and assert the true spiritual center of our culture, as Christopher Dawson used to put it. It remains to be seen whether this work can still be undertaken in Catholic universities, for reasons that are well known to us all. But I rejoice to report that it can go forward in the state schools where democracy permits everything to be pursued — even truth.

But wherever we do this work, as thinking people who strive to be faithful personally and professionally to our patrimony, as people responsible to some extent for what goes on around us, we must take whatever initiatives we can with the assurance that study fortified by prayer is invincible — or should I say, prayer implemented by study.

In one of his remarkably prophetic utterances. Alexis de Tocqueville said that "the great problem of our time is the organization and establishment of democracy in Christian lands." [20] Having done quite a bit to convert that prospect into the shabby spectacle of a de-Christianized land, may we Americans dare to entertain an even more challenging prospect for the coming century: the re-organization and re-establishment of Christianity, of Christian morality, in democrtic lands? With Belloc, Dawson, Maritain, and other prophets of a truly Christian democracy, I submit that our failure to do so will allow democracy to disappear from the land as well.[21]

Words of Orestes Brownson to the graduating class of Dartmouth in 1843 may inspire us to resume the work he so well began:

> Ask not what your age wants, but what it needs; not what it will reward, but what without which it cannot be saved; and that, go and do; do it well; do it thoroughly; and find your reward in the consciousness of having done your duty, and above all in the reflection that you have been accounted worthy to suffer somewhat for mankind.

NOTES

[1] The theme of this paper received fresh attention in my graduate seminar on religion and politics at Illinois State during the current semester. An earlier study, "The Kingdom of America versus the Kingdom of God: A Critique of the American Civil Religion" (1980), was published in part as "Modernity in the American Ideology," *Independent Journal of Philosophy*, 4 (1983) 79-87. This study grew out of an N.E.H. summer seminar at the University of California (Berkeley) in 1976 (Robert Bellah, director). The papers of Father James Schall have also been stimulating, especially **Christianity and Politics** (Boston: St. Paul Editions, 1981).

[2] The following come to mind: Walter Berns, Martin Diamond, Morton Frisch, Harry Jaffa, and scholars associated with the Claremont Institute for Statesmanship and Political Philosophy.

[3] *Communio* (Winter 1982), 292-320.

[4] (New York: Charles Scribner's Sons, 1931).

[5] (New York: Charles Scribner's Sons, 1947), p. 27.

[6] **Charles Dickens, the Last of the Great Men**, p. 12.

[7] "Very Christian Democracy," in **Christianity in Dublin** (1933).

[8] **What I Saw in America** (London: Hodder and Stoughton, 1923), especially the opening essay, "What Is America?"

[9] **We Hold These Truths: Catholic Reflections on the American Proposition** (New York: Sheed and Ward, 1960).

[10] For Niebuhr, see **The Kingdom of God in America** (New York: Harper & Row, 1937), p. 165 and passim. For the New Right, see Richard A. Viguerie, **The New Right: We're Ready to Lead** (Falls Church, Va.: The Viguerie Co., 1980), chapter VIII, "The Born-Again Christian Discovers Politics."

[11] A good selection of John Winthrop's speeches and diaries is in Perry Miller and Thomas Johnson, eds., **The Puritans**, Vol. I (New York: Harper & Row, 1963), pp. 195-209. For Junipero Serra, see documents 13 & 15 in John Tracy Ellis, ed., **Documents of American Catholic History**, Vol. I (Chicago: Henry Regnery, 1967).

[12] Madison's "Memorial and Remonstrance" (1785) and *Federalist* 51 (1788) are in Marvin Meyers, ed., **The Mind of the Founder** (Indianapolis: Bobbs-Merrill, 1973), pp. 8-16, 171-176. For Carroll, see documents 47, 48, 56 & 57 in Ellis, ed., Vol. I.

[13] Emerson's essays are in many collections of his works; especially notable are those on "Nature" and "Democracy." Brownson's most relevant work is **The American Republic: Its Constitution, Tendencies, and Destiny** (1865), ed. Americo D. Lapati (New Haven: College and University Press, 1972).

[14] I find this tendency especially evident in the writings of Michael Novak.

[15] "Statement on the Responsibilities of Citizenship," Sept. 5, 1984, para. 2.

[16] **Politics and Religious Consciousness in America** (New Brunswick, N.J.: Transaction Books, 1984), p. 247. There is a perceptive review by Timothy Fuller in *(Political Theory*, 13/1 (Feb., 1985), 145-148.

[17] (New York: Charles Scribner's Sons, 1958), p. 187 (in the section on "Religion and Civil Society").

[18] **The Naked Public Square: Religion and Democracy in America** (Grand Rapids, Mich.: Eerdmans, 1984). According to Neuhaus (as quoted by Philip F. Lawler in his review, *Catholicism in Crisis*, Oct. 1984, p. 63), "Catholics are uniquely poised to propose the American proposition anew ... by virtue of a rich tradition of social and democratic theory, and of Vatican II's theological internalization of the democratic idea. ... The Catholic moment is now. It may be missed, however."

[19] "The Conscience of the Public Catholic," *Catholicism in Crisis*, Oct., 1984, p. 51.

[20] **Democracy in America**, Vol. I (1835), J.P. Mayer, ed. (Garden City, N.Y.: Doubleday, 1969), p. 311.

[21] For Belloc, see especially "The New Paganism," in **Essays of a Catholic Layman** (1931; Freeport, N.Y.: Books for Libraries, 1967); For Dawson, "The Totalitarian State & the Christian Community," **Beyond Politics** (London: Sheed & Ward, 1939); "The Secularization of Western Culture," **The Judgement of the Nations** (1942). For Maritain, "The Gospel and the Pagan Empire," **The Twilight of Civilization** (1943).

Comments on Professor John A. Gueguen's "Public Morality in Liberal Democracy: 'E Pluribus Duo' "

by

Stephen M. Krason

I wish to begin by saying that I make these comments in the spirit of a young scholar who acknowledges that he can learn much from a senior colleague like Professor Gueguen, and so I am open to being convinced.

As things stand now, I take a somewhat different perspective than he does on a few important points. My comments focus on the nature of Protestantism, the problem of pluralism, and the role of civil or political religion, in that order.

My view of the nature and effect of Protestantism is not as harsh as Gueguen's, even though I acknowledge its error in cutting itself off from the papacy, the center of Christendom and teacher of Divine truth. This error may have led to the anthropocentric ethical tradition Gueguen says influenced America because it opened the door to other destructive ideologies. But I am not sure this tradition itself is synonymous with Protestantism, nor that it was the result of Protestantism *per se*. I believe, rather, that it was caused by secularistic movements and ideologies. These may have resulted from the *dynamic* created by Protestantism. Later, in the twentieth century, these turned around and corrupted Protestantism, as witnessed by the widespread secularization of many American Protestant denominations today.

Contrary to having an anthropocentric morality, I believe that the Protestantism prevalent in early America, which shaped our morality and law for most of our history, took its moral principles from the natural law. This was the case, possibly, because it was not that far removed in time, thought, or sentiment from its Medieval Catholic background. This was seen in the fact that our civil law in colonial times viewed the enforcement of the moral law on matters ranging from cursing to adultery as one of its primary obligations.[1] Indeed, the fact that America, as Professor Gueguen indicates, was founded in the throes of the Judeo-

Christian tradition means that it partook of the natural law tradition. (Recall constitutional scholar Edward S. Corwin explaining how the American legal-political order emerged from a "higher law" tradition going back to Plato.) [2] It is true that this nation, founded on the principles of the "new political science," departed from this tradition on some points, but did not reject it.

In seeing a flaw in the basic design of our political order, Gueguen takes a view similar to George F. Will,[3] whereas I am more inclined on this point to go along with Berns, Jaffa, et. al. to whom he refers.

Now let me speak about pluralism. While I share Gueguen's concern about how Catholic spokesmen "have been submerged in our century by a desire to accomodate the Catholic minority to the Protestant majority," I must emphasize that the problem of religious pluralism and how to deal with it remains. The solution of the secularists to this has been to remove matters of so-called "individual morality" from the law. This has been a disaster.

Rather, what is needed is a basis for law which both takes account of this pluralism (i.e., is not sectarian) and upholds the natural moral law with a correct view of human nature. I suggest that we turn to classical thought for this. This has been the approach of Leo Strauss and his followers. I believe I showed in my recent book on abortion that a reliance on ancient thinkers like Aristotle and the Stoics can take us a lot further on moral questions than a Christian thinker might initially believe.[4] This approach relies upon an acceptance of naturally-based moral norms applicable to all men. A good, brief statement of what some of these norms are appears in the appendix of C. S. Lewis' little book, **The Abolition of Man.**[5] The classics do not give us moral norms quite as high as those of Christianity, but they enable us to deal with the worst of the moral problems confronting our public policy. The Straussians have done a good job in applying these norms to the pornography/obscenity and capital punishment questions, and I was able to rely upon them in making a reasonable and fairly strong argument against all abortion.

This question might be raised: Why would Catholics want to use an approach based upon pagan ancient thought? It must be remembered that we are only talking about this as a foundation for public policy, not something to supplant our religious efforts. It enables us to solve the problem of pluralism without taking the anti-religious approach of secularism. A further advantage of this approach, in the long run, is that — given the educative force of the civil law and of public policy — it may help recreate in the U. S. the kind of perspective that will help the Church in its work of conversion. This is because it moves us away from secularism by acknowledging a transcendent order beyond man and emphasizing, as even the pagan Aristotle did, that piety is a virtue. In spite of the fact that the Jews and Athenian philosophers both resisted Christianity, it is no accident that Christianity took hold in the Mediterranean world where the way had been paved for it. Christianity united the perspectives of both Jerusalem and Athens and went beyond them. Indeed, my point is illustrated by my own experience, in which my study of classical political philosophy eventually led me to Catholic orthodoxy and theological study.

For the same reason that I am unsure about Professor Gueguen's assessment of Protestantism, I am uncertain of his assessment of America's civil or political religion. Our civil religion can have the effect, as Gueguen says, of "allow[ing] God's law to be 'temporalized,' " and maybe it actually did this. I do not believe, however, that this necessarily *had* to be the case. Indeed, genuine Judeo-Christian beliefs *do* underlie our political order, as is observed in the theistic references in the Declaration of Independence and in the insistence of statesmen like Washington, Jefferson, and Lincoln, and of Tocqueville, that our Republic needs to acknowledge God to survive. The Judeo-Christian underpinning of American political religion can and has been appealed to as a basis for opposing and redressing morally wrong public policies. Examples of this are seen in Lincoln's addresses on the slavery question and in a noteworthy speech that Senator Helms made on abortion during the August 1982 debate on the Human Life Bill.[6]

In conclusion, I believe that secularism, not Protestantism *per se,* is the cause of our current crisis of public morality. Any solution to this crisis must take account of our religious pluralism, and both classical thought and our political religion can aid us in the restoration of public morality.

NOTES

1 See Flaherty, David H., "Law and the Enforcement of Morals in Early America," in Fleming, Donald & Bailyn, Bernard, eds., **Law in American History.** (Boston: Little, Brown, 1971), p. 203.

2 See Corwin, Edward S., "The 'Higher Law' Background of American Constitutional Law," *Harvard Law Review,* Vol. 42 (1928), pp. 149, 405.

3 See Will, George F., **Statecraft As Soulcraft.** (N.Y.: Simon & Schuster, 1983).

4 See Krason, Stephen M., **Abortion: Politics, Morality, and the Constitution.** (Lanham, Md.: University Press of America, 1984).

5 See Lewis, C.S., **The Abolition of Man.** (N.Y.: Macmillan, 1947, 1955), pp. 93-121.

6 For the discussion of Lincoln on this point, see Thurow, Glen E., **Abraham Lincoln and American Political Religion.** (Albany, N.Y.: State Univ. of N.Y. Press, 1976). Helms's speech was printed in *The Wanderer,* Sept. 2, 1982, pp. 4, 7. For a discussion of Helms's speech on this point, see Krason, **ibid.,** pp. 488-493.

Two Ethical Traditions and Their Effects on Human Rights

by

Raphael T. Waters

The two moral systems mentioned by Professor Gueguen find their origins in two basic traditions, yet, as well said by Fr. Canavan, they ought not be set in opposition in view of their common basis in the word of God. The Commandments were given to the human race to help us conduct our lives as we ought to, whether as Protestants, Catholics, Jews, or Atheists.

Yet with the development of our civilization, a Protestant ethic, being based as it is in faith coupled with a corresponding anti-intellectualist attitude of some of its founders,[1] can be expected to produce some startling effects. History has not disappointed us, for we are at present experiencing antagonism to the intellectual order, an order expressed in the natural moral law. That law is the expression of how man ought to behave based upon a rational moral system which is, in turn, based upon man's nature adequately understood.[2] For human reason is the proximate measure of the morality of human behavior, but human reason, in turn, has to be measured by human nature.

Martin Luther and John Calvin were both antagonistic towards the intellectual life and can be credited with being sources of our quickening anti-intellectualism.[3] As St. Thomas Aquinas showed us with his expression of the principle of acceleration of motion, as we approach the term of any movement, we approach with an accelerating movement.[4] Hence, the quickening rejection of the intellectual basis of our moral values today gives rise to such expressions as "my set of values," with the assumption that each person has his set of values, as if they could be found dangling in the air with no intellectual or natural foundation and not necessarily like those values of another person.

But if one ignores the intellectual order or minimizes its importance in human activities, then one must logically resort to a voluntarism in moral matters. This can be seen in the great issues of our times, for the systematic development of the *science* of ethics or moral philosophy — based upon the evidence of reason — has been all but thrust aside in keeping with the general decline of the teaching of systematic philosophy.

The moral order dichotomized in its origins takes us in two directions in human affairs. On the one hand, there exists traditional moral philosophy benefitting from the guidance of moral theology.[5] On the other hand, there exists the kind of morality which ignores the natural moral law. These two directions can be seen producing their effects in two areas of importance: the political order and education.

A. The Political Order

Quite logically, once we have turned aside from natural moral law in general matters, the same must follow in the political order. For we see a strong desire for the liberal state operating for the whim and fancy of its members who find nothing *natural* in man's sociality — the assumption being that he chooses to be social purely from will. Moreover, the nature of governmental authority also finds its source in the will of the people according to popular conception and is not determined from an understanding of the common good. Thus the citizenry can demand laws and their application in whatsoever manner they desire — whence arises voluntarism, the greatest error in moral thinking.

At the same time this development is taking place, we clearly perceive the paradoxical and rapid development of the welfare society, a great step in the direction towards the absolute state.[6] The pendulum is swinging from the liberalistic social system towards the absolute state. Both are demanded by modern man. The one system, liberalism, is based upon the assumption that man is a person and a person alone with no corresponding obligations toward society. But the unfolding socialistic society assumes that man is an individual and an individual alone, replete with obligations and merely the rights accorded him by society. This is a paradox indeed: total freedom in opposition to total obligation or lack of freedom!

Maritain quite obviously saw the dangers inherent in a liberalist mentality, knowing as he did that a positivistic trend towards socialism must arise eventually. This is so because the will of the people inevitably will refuse to accept the evils which accompany complete freedom without social obligation.[7] For example, nineteenth-century liberalism has caused modern man to tend towards a social system which will redress his injustices and sufferings. The true dignity of man appears to have little consequence while the emotive order urges man to reject poverty and all kinds of injustice.

The effects of the ethical system developing out of the anti-intellectualism of the past are nowhere more keenly felt than in the economic structure of our society, wherein the term "capitalism" encompasses two opposed practices: one in keeping with a natural law view of the body economic, a second in keeping with a voluntaristic conceptualization of that same order. For, on the one hand, investments are made in order to produce goods or services while, on the other hand, investments are made to prevent others from producing goods and services. One is a socially desirable action, whereas the other is an anti-social action proceeding from a voluntaristic notion of the licitness of social activity.[8]

Professor McInerny's paper brought out the ready agreement which men find in rights without a corresponding agreement on the basis of rights. The divergence is hardly surprising since we all have certain natural inclinations urging us to seek those things which we recognize as the objects of rights. But since many men reject the basis of these rights (found proximately in reason and remotely in human nature adequately understood — some adhering to a more voluntaristic basis which eventually becomes the will of the state), it is small wonder that such a lack of agreement should exist.

The empiricist philosophy, with its attendant denial of the power of the human intellect to understand the natures of things (a stark anti-intellectualism), lies at the basis of this disagreement which is a natural consequence of the anti-intellectualist ethical background to this country's recent history.[9]

B. Education

The same paradox can be seen in the present development of educational practice. It is inevitable that once we have rejected a rational basis for ethics, a natural foundation for every rule of morals, there will be difficulty determining what education is, what it is intended to do, and how we should proceed in such matters.

Two opposed trends can be observed: one which educates man as a person (or as a whole) who exists for his own sake; and a second which considers man as an individual and merely a part, who totally exists for the sake of the society in which he lives.

As a person, the individual man is cultivated for the role of an atomized independent unit with every effort being made to facilitate his ability to make decisions. Such decisions ignore the nature of the human act which is determined by its end and the end of the agent in order to determine the morality of an act. They merely focus on the selection of the circumstances, with utter indifference to the need for norms within the social order (i.e., norms based in the nature of man and the nature of civil society). Various names are used to signify the enormous effort and funding being used to guide the minds of those being educated in this manner, names such as "sex education," "values clarification," and "E.P.I.C." (Effective Parenting Information for Children). These involve the values clarification method according to the technique established by the adherents of a secularist educational theory.[10] The names belie the true intention of the proponents of this technique — namely, to restructure the whole ethical basis of contemporary society by changing the individual's thinking.[11] The nature and function of the family, the relation between the individual and society, and the relation between the family and society are all slowly becoming a casualty to this voluntaristic educational system. Secular humanism is having its heyday with its situation ethics and its outright denial of the existence of God, Who is a necessary point of reference for any ethical theory.

At the same time that this liberalistic rugged individualism is being inculcated into the value system of the child, the steady development of the absolute state is taking place. For, as can be expected, parental authority is being undermined in favor of the state, which is fast assuming authority in all matters educational.[12]

Here we have the same paradox: an educational system which ostensibly tries to develop an independent child as if he were a person, a responsible whole (the whole process having a voluntaristic basis), while, at the same time, the child is assumed into the state system as a mere part with utter dependence on the State. Expendability becomes the key concept, as anyone familiar with the values clarification method discovers in the literature coercing children into absurd science fiction case histories. The public good is to be preserved at all costs: even the elimination of the incurables, the unwanted (mere fetuses!), the deformed, and the elderly. Thus man has gone from being a person to a mere individual, a whole to a part, with the latter either a useful or a useless citizen!

Small wonder then that those seeking agreement on human rights have difficulty agreeing on the basis of such rights when the doctrinal differences are so great, arising as they do from a diverse understanding of the whole order of human operations. These bases would appear to be irreconcilable in the same way as opposed religious doctrines appear irreconcilable. The imposition of will in place of the intellectual order can only be reversed with the discovery of a unified rational vision of reality. Failing that, human rights, without a sure foundation, can only be placed in jeopardy with a consequent loss of freedom for each man.

NOTES

[1] Thomas Neill, **Makers of the Modern Mind,** Milwaukee, Bruce, 1949, Ch. II-III.

[2] Thomas Higgins, **Man as Man. the Science and Art of Ethics,** rev. ed., Milwaukee, Bruce, 1958, pp. 64-68.

[3] Thomas Neill, **Op. cit.,** Ch. II, III.

[4] St. Thomas Aquinas, **S.C.G.** III, Ch. XV, n. 13.

[5] Raphael Waters, "The Relationship of Moral Philosophy to Moral Theology," in *Listening,* Vol. 18, No. 3, Fall, 1983, pp. 235-244.

[6] Hilaire Belloc, **The Servile State,** London, Constable and Company, 1927.

[7] Jacques Maritain, **Scholasticism and Politics,** 2nd. ed., London, Geoffrey Bles, 1945, pp. 55, 75-77; **The Person and the Common Good,** New York, Charles Scribner's Sons, 1947, p. 82.

[8] Raphael Waters, "The Two Faces of Capitalism," in *Social Justice Review,* July-August, 1984.

[9] See especially the works of John Locke and David Hume, two classic English empiricists.

[10] Theodore Brameld, "A Reconstructionist View of Education," in **Philosophies of Education,** New York, John Wiley and Sons, 1961, pp. 104-111; Sidney B. Simon and Sally Wendkos Olds, **Helping Your Child Learns Right from Wrong,** New York, McGraw-Hill, 1976, p. 12; Louis E. Raths, et. al., **Values and Teaching,** 2nd. ed., Columbus, Charles E. Merrill, 1978, Ch. 1-3; Onalee McGraw, **Secular Humanism and the Schools: the Issue Whose Time Has Come,** Washington, The Heritage Foundation, 1976, pp. 4-12; Paul C. Vitz, **Psychology as Religion,** Grand Rapids, Michigan, William B. Eerdmans, 1977, pp. 108-114.

[11] Theodore Brameld, **Ibid.**
Onalee McGraw, **The Family, Feminism and the Therapeutic State,** Washington, D.C., The Heritage Foundation, 1980, pp. 2, 13, 14-16, 30-33, 56-63; John Goodlad, "Report of Task Force C," in *Schooling for the Future.* A Report to *the President's Commission on School Finance,* Los Angeles, California, Education Inquiry, Inc., October 15, 1971, p. 14; Vince Nesbitt, **Humanistic Morals and Values in Education,** Lane Cove, Sydney, Australia, 1981, passim; Kenneth S. Kenworthy, **Social Studies for the Seventies,** Waltham, Massachusetts, Ginn and Company, 1969, pp. 245, 254.

[12] C. Stephen Hathcock, "With the Graceys," in *Triumph,* January, 1971; Blair Adams and Joel Stein, **Who Owns the Children? Compulsory Education and the Dilemma of Ultimate Authority,** 2nd. ed., Grand Junction, Colorado, Truth Forum, 1984, (Education as Religious War, Book Five), especially Chapters 2 and 3.

Two Moral Theologians

by

G. E. M. Anscombe

Vermeersch's treatise on lying is interesting and learned. The greater part of it is devoted to telling us what other people have thought. With one exception, I'll not be referring to this. Vermeersch makes clear from the first that his intention, or what he thinks is his intention, is to defend the classical absolute condemnation of lying. Thus he, in particular, rejects the view that lying is to be condemned because of the social harms involved in or resulting from it. "An act which of its nature corrupts the one instrument of social communication, which hinders human commerce, nay tends to the overthrow of human society" does seem to contain a grave disorder: but in saying this we ought not to forget that lying *as such* — i.e., just any lie, whatever further characteristics it has — is not eo ipso a grave sin. Besides, the deduction from consequences is extrinsic and ineffective for the condemnation of *all* lying, for there are lies which can be socially useful.

He compares lying to contraception, both being unnatural acts. Speech is the one means of communication among human beings. Mankind should form a unity, but human nature is divided among indefinitely many individuals and can never exist as an *actual whole,* because there can always be more men. So men must be *brought* to a sort of unity and made as it were into *one whole man* by *caritativa communicatio.* Original sin, however, and its consequences prevent this, though our nature inclines us to mutual communication, as is evidenced both in the native simplicity of a child and in the shame of being detected in a lie by the person you are lying to.

What Vermeersch wants to show is that the "order of mutual communication" is *inviolable* for the human race. It follows that a man cannot honestly subordinate that order to himself, but ought to fear (I suppose he means reverence) it as part of an essential order.

But we must ask: what is an "essential" order and when is it violated? There isn't always evil when the order of something is violated — else we'd sin in eating eggs. There is sin in the violation of an order (ordo) *to which we are subordinate.* Grave sin isn't the particular violation of just any ordo, but of *the essential ordo* to which that particular one relates. The ordo of speech is a particular one which relates to charity. And so it comes about that although a lie is contrary to the ordo of speech, still it isn't *against,* only *outside* (praeter) the order of charity. That is to say, it allows *that* order to be substantially intact. In short, you aren't violating charity by lying to someone, not by any old lie, but only by a lie out of hatred or a lie about which there is something you have an obligation to tell. This is so, according to Vermeersch, in spite of the fact that the point of speech is 'caritative communication' and *because* this lying is always wrong. His conclusion seems admirable, but his thinking here is a bit odd. If the order of speech is inviolable because and only because speech relates to the "order of charity," how is it that that doesn't show that lying is always wrong and that it is always a violation of the "order of charity?" Or, if it is not always a violation of the "order of charity," how does its relation to the order of charity manage to show that it is *always* wrong? I am not disputing his conclusion that lying is always wrong but not always mortally sinful. I am only criticizing the reasons he offers for this conclusion.

He proceeds to deal with the case in which it is justified or positive-required *not* to tell someone something when he is asking you about it. Here Vermeersch is highly critical of the idea of *restrictio mentalis.* This is the idea that in order not to be lying — i.e., producing speech contrary to your own mind — you restrict your *meaning* to that meaning of the ambiguous expression in which it is true. This idea is infected by the notion of an act of meaning (i.e., the notion that you have to be *thinking* about meaning something in order to be meaning it and not the other thing). Whereas I would suppose that you only had to think, if at all, "Well, it's true in *that* sense, anyway," the question at issue is whether the fact that you hope and intend that the hearer will take it in the sense in which it is false means that you are telling a lie.

However, it is not my business here to defend the position in question but to point to the very singular device of Vermeersch in reaching *the conclusion that you aren't* lying. His first observation is the obvious one that not all speech is assertion. This is not because speech may be questions, orders, complaints, and so on. No, his point is that speech may have the form of assertion but not be assertion because, for example, it is uttered by an actor on a stage or because it is a joke. No one will say the actor or storyteller is lying, says Vermeersch. True enough, and something like that is true about jokes. He now makes the most amazing assertions himself, which, alas, are not *jokes.* If someone is asked whether he has committed adultery, and he says no, what this means is *not* the assertion that he hasn't, it means: either he hasn't, or he doesn't want to admit it.

Now how much is there in this? Take a criminal act. It may be a formality that you plead not guilty; so much so that if you refuse to plead, a plea of not guilty is automatically entered by the court. *That,* it can reasonably be argued, puts an interpretation on your plea of not guilty when you do make it though you think you know you *are* guilty. This I think we can accept. But that generally you can say that something is the case which is not and *that* not be a lie, not because of ambiguity but because you *aren't* asserting it, is much worse nonsense than some of the contentions of the mental restrictioners were.

Now this influential piece by Vermeersch has an interesting family resemblance to the presently very influential book by Bruno Schuller entitled **Die Begrundung der Sittliche Urteile.**

When I began to read Schuller's book, I was amazed. I knew it was influential, but I could not see how it could be regarded as anything but ridiculous. This is because of the way it begins. To put briefly what Schuller spends a lot of ink on: he has noticed that the ten command-ments are not statements, but commandments. He produces a word 'Paranese,' which he first explains as covering orders and prohibitions and warnings and encouragements. This is well and good: it may be useful to have such a word. In English, we are used to discussing "imper-atives," which I suppose covers much the same ground, though an imperative is also used for advice. But Schuller has a rhetorical reason for introducing an unfamiliar word; he wishes to characterize the 'paraenetic' in a way which shall be very directive for moral philosophy.

The fact that a commandment is not a statement but a command or prohibition is confused in his mind with a non-fact — viz., that it has no non-tautological content. So, commenting on the first two command-ments, he writes: "Keep holy the Sabbath day; rest on it." "Sabbath day," he says, may mean "rest day" and that would mean "day on which you ought to rest." So the commandment means "Rest on the day on which you ought to rest." Translate that into a statement and you get: "You ought to rest on the day on which you ought to rest." The remain-ing commandments get the same treatment. "Honor your father and mother." Well, what does "father and mother" mean? Not what you might think: it means "Respect people you ought to respect." "Thou shalt not kill," he tells us, means "Thou shalt not kill wrongfully." For, he says, people who know Hebrew tell us that the Hebrew word translated "kill" means "wrongful killing" or "murder." One understands that they are a bit short of rabbis in Germany these days; but I fear Schuller didn't even try to consult any rabbis. My own experience is that if you ask a Jew who knows Hebrew well, he will tell you that the word is not the ordinary word for killing; you'd use another word for killing in war and another for the work of a butcher. (I have not had the idea — till just now — of seeing whether a word for killing is used in connection with what the 'avenger of blood' might do, or which word is used for what you would have done if you had killed someone accidentally and had to flee to one of the cities of refuge to escape the avenger of blood). What I was told was that the word used in the commandment covers what in England we call "manslaughter" as well as what we call "murder." That this shows it *means* "wrongful killing" may be maintained by some people, but this meaning is surely false. An executioner who knowingly executed his own father would thereby be guilty of *wrongful killing* but not of either murder or manslaughter.[1] So "wrongful killing" is more *"extensive,"* as Vermeersch would say, than "murder" or "murder-and-manslaughter."

The commandments against stealing, false witness, and adultery get the same sort of treatment.

We are given a *general* thesis about "ethical exhortation or Paranese." Schuller confines *his* application of Paranese to the ethical. He writes: "An important indication (for such sentences) is that if, contrary to their own intention, they are construed as propositions communicating knowledge, they assume the form of tautologies or empty formulae." Of course, he *sees* to it that they do so, by reinterpreting them.

I can not understand how people could be snowed by such writing. What suppression of what they knew can make them accept that "father and mother" doesn't mean father and mother? How can they suppose that that commandment which contains the week in it — "Six days shall thou labour and do all that thou hast to do," as it enjoins rest on the seventh day — can come out as tautology if transformed into a "You ought to" proposition? It is true, as Schuller remarks, that a commandment against adultery could not be given to people who had no institution of marriage; equally a commandment against theft presupposes some custom of property. It is true, then, that disapproval of theft and adultery is also to some degree presupposed. I learned from a Jewish surgeon that the traditional vital application of "Honor your father and mother" was not to leave them to die by the wayside in the desert travel of the children of Israel. Schuller thinks that anything he calls "paraenetic" conforms to an already totally and utterly unquestioningly received morality. Well, he can restrict his term like that if he likes; it is then not open to him to assume that the ten commandments were what he calls "paraenetic." This sliding in of something which, given the way in which

---

[1] I owe this observation to Dr. M. C. Geach.

a term has been introduced, may very well not be so, is, I fear, characteristic.

Reading the rest of the book I perceived why, having somehow swallowed or skipped this first chapter, people might be impressed. The book is learned especially in Anglo-American moral philosophy. However, the purpose of the first chapter becomes clear: it provides a very fundamental defense against the protest that we *know* certain things are required, certain others wrong. We know this from the commandments.

As I said, there is a curious resemblance to Vermeersch. To justify themselves, both moral theologians play Humpty Dumpty with words and use well-known facts, which makes their topics even more difficult than a naive person would think. There, however, the similarity ends: Vermeersch *thinks* he is strictly maintaining a strict doctrine; Schuller's bent is to make hay of any strict doctrine.

Schuller's book is also quite interesting reading. But you have to be watchful. He writes *as if* there were only two possibilities when there are evidently, or likely to be, more. About lying, for example, he writes that if one must preserve a secret and is asked a question about it when "silence will betray," one must *either* lie *or give an answer* which *is* an answer but which doesn't betray. In giving such an answer, one uses a restrictive concept of lying so that what one says, by this concept, doesn't count as a lie. Schuller's comment is that the restriction imposed on the concept of lying brings the people who are supposedly "deontological" near to what he calls a "teleological" view. If I am to translate this, it seems to mean: (a) that this restriction *is* justified by the good result of not betraying the secret; and (b) that the alleged purpose, *not to lie*, is a put-up job. But the effort to give an account of how one can give an answer and yet avoid a lie seems to distinguish such a person from a "teleologist," if the latter judges one should be willing to lie for the good purpose.

Schuller explains the contrast between "deontologists" and "teleologists." A "teleologist" thinks that all actions are to be judged only by their consequences; and a "deontologist" (of the more savage sort) thinks that some actions are wrong no matter what the consequences. The milder sort of 'deontologist' thinks that *all* actions are to be judged always *partly*, but not always only by their consequences. Schuller maintains the "teleological" ethics is the right Catholic sort.

In any case, I can say: there *is* a crucial difference between moral philosophers in regard to what they think of as kinds of action one should not do for an advantage to be gained or an evil to be avoided. I say one should lie about the thing *rather* than give the fugitive away. How come?

Isn't that doing something bad for the sake of avoiding an evil — viz., the evil of the fugitive being caught? This must be what incites Schuller to say that the devices invented to show what would *not* be a lie come as near as anything to teleology.

People may easily be incited to say that the devices invented to show that something would *not* be a lie come as near as you like to saying — "Lie for the good purpose, or to avoid the evil, and I'll tell you a way of muddling your mind into thinking it isn't a lie." Now *aren't* we just judging by consequences here?

No, and the point is important. If it is absolutely clear that someone can't be persuaded to avoid wrongdoing altogether in some matter, it is good to persuade him to commit some lesser sin than what he is minded to do. If you *cannot* see any alternative to committing one sin or another, you act better if you choose the lesser sin, And you may not have time of cleverness to discover a better possibility. To betray the fugitive, we will suppose, is a gravely wicked thing to do. Telling the pursuers his location *is* betraying him. So, in this case, telling that truth is a wicked act — more than telling the lie that he is not there. But suppose that somebody else threatened that he would give the fugitive away unless you told some lie? Though the case is different, a consequentialist would apply the same principle. If you are a consequentialist, you are likely to say you should tell that lie just as much as the other one. But I didn't say you *should* tell the other one, only that you should do it *rather* than commit an act of betrayal by what you tell the pursuers. If you are a consequentialist you will hold that you are responsible for all the consequences of your acts and omissions and, therefore, that you are responsible for the capture of the fugitive if he were caught because you refused to tell the lie demanded by the person who betrayed him — just as much as if you betrayed him.

Now I am not quite clear to what extent Schuller is a consequentialist. He sometimes forgets the totality of opinion involved in defining the "teleologist." A "teleologist" thinks *all* acts are determined in their moral character by their consequences or tendency to produce certain consequences. Conversely, the people who are "deontologists" think there are some *kinds* of acts that are wicked regardless of their consequences. As a "teleologist" is one who holds the view that contradicts this, he thinks there are not such *kinds* of acts. This would seem to lead to his thinking that if any particular act is wicked, it is not as being of such and such a *kind*.

Now Schuller objects to attacks by "deontologists" on "teleologists" which run like this: "Am I to defraud someone because I could do better things with the money I owe him, than by giving it to him? If you go by consequences only, justice and fairness go overboard." With that justification, asks Schuller, are justice and fairness not to be counted among the consequences of your act? Schuller certainly is given to making rather unimpressive statements of opposing positions. However, this is a very interesting one. If you do pay what you owe, justice is satisfied as far as that transaction is concerned. So that's part of the consequences. And it may outweigh the advantage of what you might have done with the money. But what if it doesn't? Well, it's not clear that you intend the permanent defrauding of the other party. So, if some really serious need for the money here and now makes you say "Sorry, can't pay you today," justice isn't flouted: its demands are merely postponed. Will that be objectionable?

Well, what we want is not such a case. We want a case where the consequences of a lie, or of an intentional adultery, or of deliberately killing a baby, are held by a teleologist to justify the action (i.e., to make it out to have been a good action in spite of its having one of those characters). Why I use lying as an example ought to be clear from what I have said in the matter of betraying the fugitive. We ought not to take a case where one of the things would at any rate be *less bad* than any alternative you can think of. "Such," you might say, "can always be imagined." But, no, it would be too fanciful to think out a case where you are irresistibly tempted either to commit adultery *or* murder, so you choose the adultery as the lesser sin. You can only introduce cases plausibly if you construct a set-up such that this action will have such and such consequences and refusing to do it will mean those consequences won't occur. Let the consequences be greatly desirable, the to-be-expected alternative dreadful and miserable; nevertheless is the weight of the badness of the act something to put into the calculus of the total value or disvalue of the consequences — as Schuller in effect says justice and fairness would be?

Moore argued that everyone has to be a consequentialist — has to accept his analysis of the rightness and wrongness of an action. For, he says, your action must have consequences, and, if you say they don't matter, what you *have to* mean is that the sum of their value is never such as to outweigh the sum of disvalue when the act is intrinsically evil. Moore says that anyone who thinks of ethics at all must think this, and, in this way, he accomodates to his own general theory the views of those who say, e.g., "Deliberately procuring abortion is wrong whatever the consequences. You must not do that."

If Moore is right, then the differences between a "deontologist" and a "teleologist" is ill-expressed by contrasting the views so labelled: it would be a matter of including or not including the value or disvalue of an act under a certain description in the sum of the value and disvalue of consequences. Or, more seriously, the difference might be between people who think that the disvalue of an intrinsically wrong act is *eo ipso* so great that it could not be outweighed, and those who think that no kind of act is in that sense intrinsically wrong. As Schuller seems to think there is a serious difference and that the right ethic is "teleological," it follows that he is among those who do not think any kind of action is intrinsically wrong and so irredeemable. Moreover, Schuller's thesis that traditional Catholic morality is "teleological" is a startling imprudence.

Comparing Vermeersch and Schuller, I have found a certain likeness between them in their Humpty Dumpty with words. Schuller plays with words to anaesthetise his readers against the effects of knowing the ten commandments; Vermeersch to justify lying in response to unwelcome interrogation. While Vermeersch thinks he is maintaining a strict classical doctrine that lying is always wrong, he may seem rather to contrast with Schuller who does not desire even an appearance of holding an absolutist position. However, as I hope to have shown, the absolutism of Vermeersch is something of a self-deception.

Let us turn to another topic to show Vermeersch in his world-pleasing role. He discusses killing in self-defense. He is admirable in his criticism of the "principle of double effect" in St. Thomas' article on this subject (**Summa Theologica** II IIae, Q64, art. 7). St. Thomas thinks that even in self-defense one may not kill on purpose: "Illicitum est quod homo intendat occidere ut se defendat." St. Thomas' rigorous doctrine has its difficulties. If in a struggle on the edge of a cliff you push your assailant over the edge, it is reasonable to say you are intentionally exerting enough force to push him away from you and so it may well be true that you didn't intend his death. But suppose you shoot and kill him? (Or, to make the point more strongly, you throw a hand grenade which is all you've got to repel one who is advancing on you with a machine gun?) "How," asks Vermeersch, "is the killing of the aggressor not direct (i.e., not chosen as a means to saving yourself?)" Here he makes a suggestion which is worth careful thought:

> "The unjust aggression itself morally alters the action of exploding (shooting) the gun. Without that present attack, the explosion (shooting) of the gun neither would nor could be anything but a direct killing. But now that aggression, persisting for some time, makes it fall under the concept of defense, and of a defense the intention of which is directed to saving yourself. This shows why actual (present) attack has to be stipulated among the conditions of bloody defense. For when the actual attack stops, the action would simply fall under the concept of killing for an end, perhaps a good end: but it isn't permissible to do evil for the sake of good."

If the main thing Vermeersch means by this passage is respectable, it can't be that in such a case you are justified because you *aren't* engaged in intentional direct killing. I would rather understand him as saying that an attack which makes your shooting fall under the concept (gives it the *ratio*) of immediate defense is a counter-example to the prohibition of "direct" (i.e., intentional) killing. This is worthy of more exploration.

I fear, however, that he meant worse. As in the case of lying, he thought he was adhering to a classically rigorous principle. But look how he goes on:

> But there is no lack of other examples in which an action, physically very clearly direct, is nevertheless held to be morally purely permissive, because it goes with another physical effectiveness, which alone is intended. Thus, as everybody admits, the burning of innocent people is merely being permitted by one 'who burns innocents in a tower along with nocents ... because by the intention of the agent the action only looks to the burning of the nocents, although here and now the burning of these cannot be separated from the burning of the others'; thus someone who transfixes a nocent by piercing an innocent placed between is judged neither to have intended nor to have chosen the killing of that innocent. In the same way the unjust attack here conferred a double immediate effectiveness on the explosion of the gun: one being the defense of the man being attacked, which alone is chosen and intended, the other the killing, which is only being permitted.

This doctrine is introduced for the sake of an application to lying. Vermeersch continues:

> Someone who requires us to disclose a matter we have a right to keep secret is an unjust aggressor: materially or formally so, according as he is or is nor conscious of his importunity. This makes no difference, as it is all right to repel an attack with the same kind of defense, whether it is materially or formally blameworthy. ... In themselves, the words would be nothing but a signification of what is false. But the unjust attack of the other has the effect that they are at the same time a defense of oneself. Where they are so applied, the false signification is merely permitted. Hence the fault of lying is absent in our case, for the same reason as the concept of homicide does not apply in the other.

I would have to know more history than I do in order to say whether Vermeersch is sounding a new note. Certainly, the earlier casuistry on the subject of lying seemed to me to have been inspired by a traditional concern that one does not sin against the truth, which is what assertion is for (For this last, see St. Anselm, **De Veritate** cap. II). This concern appears in Vermeersch only as a concern that one finds a legal loophole to get out of a charge of lying. As for the matters he adduces as parallels, they seem sinister indeed. Perhaps they were already there in a tradition in which he writes. Whether this is so or not, there is a strong atmosphere of one using his quite powerful talents to go along with the world, to reassure and to flatter it. This characteristic is raised to a higher degree in Schuller's **Die Begrundung Sittliche Urteile.**

Infallibility and Specific Moral Norms: A Reply to Francis A. Sullivan, S.J.

by

Germain Grisez

Francis A. Sullivan, S.J., who for many years has been professor of ecclesiology at the Gregorian University in Rome, recently published an important book on the magisterium. While I agree with much of Sullivan's theology of the magisterium, I take issue with certain aspects of his argument in chapter six: "The Infallibility of the Ordinary Magisterium and the Limits of the Object of Infallibility."

There Sullivan criticizes a position John C. Ford, S.J., and I defended in our article in the June 1978 *Theological Studies:* that the received Catholic teaching on contraception (and, by implication, on many other questions about sex, marriage, and innocent life) has been taught infallibly by the ordinary magisterium. Sullivan maintains that no specific moral norm can be taught infallibly. In this paper, I will show that he has neither refuted our position nor established his.

During the controversy following **Humanae vitae**, it was widely assumed that, since the encyclical contains no solemn definition, the teaching it reaffirms is not proposed infallibly and could be mistaken. That assumption simply ignored the entire category of teachings infallibly proposed by the ordinary magisterium. However, in **Dei filius**, Vatican I definitively teaches that there is such a category (DS 3011/ 1792). And Vatican II articulates criteria for the infallibility of the ordinary magisterium:

> Although the bishops individually do not enjoy the prerogative of infallibility, they nevertheless proclaim the teaching of Christ infallibly, even when they are dispersed throughout the world, provided that they remain in communion with each other and with the successor of Peter and that in authoritatively teaching on a matter of faith and morals they agree in one judgment as that to be held definitively. (LG 25)

Reflecting on Vatican II's formulation, Ford and I became convinced that the received teaching on contraception meets the criteria. We clarified the conditions for the infallible exercise of the ordinary magisterium by tracing the development of Vatican II's text in the conciliar proceedings. We then argued that the facts show that the received Catholic teaching on contraception has met these conditions.

In making our case, we did not try to show that the norm concerning contraception pertains to revelation because Vatican II does not include that among the criteria by which infallible teachings of the ordinary magisterium are to be recognized. However, in specifying the limits of infallibility in defining, the Council states: "Now this infallibility, with which the divine Redeemer willed his Church to be endowed in defining a doctrine of faith or morals, extends as far as extends the deposit of divine revelation, which must be guarded as inviolable and expounded with fidelity" (LG 25). This statement of the limits of infallibility makes it clear that, if anything is taught infallibly, it must pertain to revelation, at least by being a truth required to safeguard and develop revelation itself.

The connection is essential. But it does not follow that no teaching can be recognized as infallible without first being recognized as pertaining to revelation. Essential conditions for a reality need not be conditions for recognizing instances of that kind of reality. For instance, water is H_2O, but one can recognize instances of water without first knowing them to be H_2O. Similarly, the fact that a moral teaching within the infallible competence of the magisterium must either be revealed or closely connected with revelation need not prevent one from first recognizing instances of such points of morals and only thereby coming to know that they *somehow* pertain to revelation.

Therefore, Ford and I proceeded on the assumption that, if a teaching meets the conditions articulated by Vatican II, it can be recognized as infallibly proposed, it can be known to pertain to revelation. The question of how it pertains is secondary. Still, since the connection between infallibility and revelation is essential, if the norm concerning contraception has been proposed infallibly, this secondary question is important. Thus we treated it first in a series of subordinate questions and objections.

In beginning our account of the way in which the norm concerning contraception pertains to revelation, we expected the objection: Your argument is going in the wrong direction; you ought first to have shown how this teaching pertains to revelation, and then how the Church has taught it. That objection would have been based on the supposition: nothing can be recognized as pertaining to revelation from the manner in which the Church holds and hands it on. A single counterexample falsifies a general thesis, so we offered one counterexample: the dogma of the Assumption and the argument Pius XII offered for its being revealed when he defined it.

Instead of beginning his criticism of Ford's and my position by examining our basic argument, Sullivan starts with our treatment of the subordinate question. He says that, when we refer to the doctrine of the Assumption, we are trying to prove by analogy that the morality of contraception is a proper object for the infallible magisterium. But a counter-example is not an argument by analogy, so the disanalogies do not tell against Ford's and my point. One can legitimately argue from the way the Church holds and teaches something to its pertaining to revelation; one need not show that something pertains to revelation; or how it pertains, to recognize it as an integral part of the Church's teaching.

Sullivan reformulates what he takes to be the supposition of our argument: "If the magisterium speaks in a definitive way about something, it must necessarily be the case that what they speak about is a proper object of infallible teaching." He says this supposition "would eliminate the possibility of challenging any magisterial act that was claimed to be infallible by questioning whether the subject-matter of that act fell within the limits of the proper object of infallibility" (144). Sullivan says:

> Against such a view I would argue that, if it were true, there would be no point at all in the insistence of Vatican I and Vatican II that the magisterium can speak infallibly only on matters of faith and morals. It would have been necessary to say only this: whenever the magisterium speaks in a definitive way it must be speaking infallibly, because the very fact that it speaks in a definitive way would guarantee that what it speaks about would be a proper matter for infallible teaching.   (144-45)

Thus Sullivan claims that Ford and I are arguing that we can only know for certain that the morality of contraception is a *proper object* for infallible teaching from the fact that the magisterium has taught it infallibly.

In reply, I distinguish: we do say that the only way to prove conclusively that this teaching either pertains to revelation or is closely connected with it — and in *this* sense is a proper object of infallible teaching — is the fact that the magisterium has proposed it infallibly. But we do not say that the only way to recognize the teaching as a matter of "faith or morals" — and in *this* sense as falling within the magisterium's competence as a *potential* object of an infallible teaching — is the fact that the magisterium has proposed it infallibly.

Sullivan equivocates; his argument succeeds only on the assumption that "faith and morals" in **Lumen gentium,** 25, really means "a point of faith or morals *known* to pertain to revelation." This assumption of Sullivan's is the general thesis Ford and I showed to be false by the example of the doctrine of the Assumption. And there is another way of seeing that Sullivan's assumption is mistaken.

Christians always have believed that the apostles and their successors bonded together in communion enjoy an unfailing charism of truth. That is why, when disputes arose concerning what really is revealed truth, appeals were made to what had been held and handed down in all the churches. The force of that appeal never depended on an independent showing that the truth in question was revealed. That condition, which Sullivan wishes to impose, would have blocked the attempt to proceed from the way truths are held and handed on to their status as pertaining to revelation.

Ford and I offered an argument that the norm concerning contraception is a matter of morals: "Vatican II itself, in **Gaudium et spes**, 51, at least affirmed the competency of the magisterium in this very matter when it stated: 'Relying on these principles, it is not allowed that children of the Church in regulating procreation shoud use methods which are disapproved of by the magisterium in its explaining of the divine law.' " We thought that "in its explaining of the divine law" shows that the morality of contraception falls under "faith or morals."

Sullivan himself grants that the magisterium can speak authoritatively on particular moral issues. To show this, he quotes a few texts, including Vatican II's statement that in the matter of birth regulation parents "must always be governed according to a conscience dutifully conformed to the divine law itself, and should be submissive toward the Church's teaching office, which authentically interprets that law in the light of the gospel" (138, GS 50). But Sullivan thinks that no specific moral norm can be taught infallibly.

That opinion emerged only since Vatican II. Sullivan himself implies as much, for when he first raises the question, "How much of the natural law is also revealed?" he proposes the view which excludes specific moral norms as "the strong trend in current moral thinking" (137). he concludes the chapter by treating with approval the opinion, which he thinks is that of the majority of Catholic moral theologians today, that "particular norms of natural law are not objects of infallible teaching" (148).

The current opinion Sullivan embraces denies the possibility of moral absolutes as such, not merely the moral norm concerning contraception. The challenge extends to other questions about sex, marriage, and innocent life. In the new theory, "Thou shalt not commit adultery" is always a correct norm of Christian life only if "adultery" is understood to mean *wrongful* extramarital intercourse. The theory is that no "material" norm — that is, no norm without a built in moral characterization of the act it concerns — can possibly hold always and everywhere. From this it would follow, of course, that no such norm can be an unchanging truth, and so no such norm can be proposed infallibly.

Now, since it was commonly supposed until after Vatican II that revelation does include specific moral norms, it is reasonable to take "faith and morals" in the Council's documents as including reference to such norms. To take the conditions which Vatican II articulated for the infallible exercise of the ordinary magisterium as if they included the restriction Sullivan tries to impose is to replace the view the Council Fathers took for granted with a different view which they had never thought of. I do not say that such a replacement would *contradict* the Council's formal teaching. But one cannot simply read it into the Council's formulation.

Sullivan needs some cogent theological grounds for setting this limit to "morals." He tries to find such support mainly in Vatican I.

Sullivan claims that there is "evidence that the term *res fidei et morum* was not understood at Vatican I to embrace all possible questions of natural morality" (140). He adduces this evidence when he rejects an argument for the view that the magisterium can teach specific moral norms infallibly: "The magisterium is infallible in matters of faith and morals: but particular norms of the natural law are matters of morals; therefore the magisterium can speak infallibly about them." Sullivan rejects this as "rather simplistic" because "it ignores the difference between what is revealed and what is not revealed with regard to moral."

By itself, this statement of Sullivan's would merely repeat what he needs to prove. So he seeks to establish the point by appealing to Bishop Gasser's response to a proposal to substitute "principles of morals" for *res morum* in the definition of papal infallibility. Sullivan cites the second of two reasons why the **Deputatio de fide** rejected this proposal: "Moreover, principles of morals can be other merely philosophical principles of natural morality *(alia mere philosophica naturalis honestatis)* which do not in every respect pertain to the deposit of faith" (140). Sullivan thinks this portion of Gasser's comment an "illuminating proof" of his thesis.

However, the first reason Gasser gives for rejecting the proposed amendment is an even more illuminating disproof of Sullivan's thesis:

> But the **Deputatio de fide** cannot accept this amendment either, partly because that expression would be wholly new, while the expression *res fidei et morum* for doctrine of faith and morals is very well known, and every theologian knows what ought to be understood by these words.
> (**Mansi**, 52:1224)

The theological periti of Vatican I plainly knew what every theologian knew. J. Kleutgen and J. B. Franzelin were leading *periti* of Vatican I; both participated in the session of the **Deputatio de fide** where Gasser's responses to the proposed amendment were determined (53:270-72). But Sullivan himself says that these two theologians were among those who "asserted that the whole of the natural law is revealed, without making any distinction between the basic principles and more particular norms" (137; 226). Thus, theologians Gasser knew well included specific moral norms under "faith and morals."

Had Vatican I accepted the amendment which was thus rejected, Sullivan would have had some real support. For the amendment, proposed by Archbishop Yusto of Burgos, was intended to restrict the scope of the infallible teaching authority to principles in order to exclude moral determinations which depend on matters of fact that are not revealed (52:854). But this argument, which is close to Sullivan's, must not have seemed cogent to the **Deputatio de fide**, for they rejected Yusto's proposed amendment.

But if Gasser's remarks cannot be read as excluding specific moral norms from the object of the infallible magisterium marked out by the phrase "faith and morals," what could the **Deputatio de fide** have meant by "merely philosophical principles of natural morality, which do not in every respect pertain to the deposit of faith"? I think a clue to the answer is in the phrase "naturalis honestatis," which Sullivan translates "natural morality." The translation is not bad, but it facilitates Sullivan's argument in a way that the Latin does not. For "naturalis honestatis" does not mean the same thing as "naturalis legis," and the two expressions have different connotations.

"Honestas" does refer to morality, but it means moral uprightness (not moral goodness *or* badness), and it connotes the social value of upright character which merits honor. There is a body of philosophical moral literature concerned with *honestas.* It includes, for instance, Castiglione's **Courtier** and Chesterfield's **Letters to His Son**. This genre mixes morals in the strict sense with social conventions, etiquette, and practical techniques for getting ahead. The philosophical principles *naturalis honestatis* found in works of this genre might be included in the reference of "principles of morals." But, for the most part, such "principles of morals" have little to do with the deposit of faith. They pertain to it only to the extent that they touch on matters of faith and morals. For example, when Chesterfield explains how to conduct extramarital affairs discretely, the immorality of fornication and adultery pertains to the deposit of faith, but the honorable way of engaging in that immorality does not.

When Gasser spoke of "alia mere philosophica naturalis honestatis, quae non sub omni respectu pertinent ad depositum fidei," he may well have meant principles of morals of that sort. In any case, the first reply to the proposed amendment, which Sullivan ignores, makes it clear that "faith and morals" in Vatican I means what every theologian at the time meant by it — what Kleutgen meant by it.

What Vatican I meant by "morals" is extremely important because that Council used "faith and morals" in specifying the authority of the pope teaching *ex cathedra,* and in its definition Vatican I identified the object of papal infallibility with that of the Church. Thus, Vatican I implicitly defined the infallibility of the Church as extending to matters of "morals." And this implicit definition should be taken to mean what Vatican I in fact meant by it. But Vatican I included in the reference of "morals" what theologians of that time included — specific moral norms. It follows that the reference of "faith and morals" in Vatican I's implicit definition of the infallibility of the Church ought to be taken to include specific moral norms.

But if they bow to the evidence that Vatican I included specific moral norms in the reference of "faith and morals," those who wish to exclude such specific norms from the object of infallibility will argue that Vatican I has not definitively rejected their position. Since all theologians at the time thought the Church could teach infallibly on such questions, this was not then at issue. Hence, the Council did not consider this issue, and so the common theological view of the time cannot have settled it.

I grant (not concede) that Vatican I did not definitively teach that the Church's competence to teach infallibly extends to specific moral norms. Still, Ford's and my view that contraception falls under "faith and morals" as the phrase is used by Vatican I and Vatican II in their statements of conditions for infallible teaching finds support in the documents, while Sullivan's contrary view finds none.

Furthermore, by citing passages in four previous documents as comparable to its own teaching, Vatican II itself provides guidance on the correct interpretation of the conditions for infallible teaching by the ordinary magisterium. One of the documents cited as Vatican I's revised schema for the second constitution **De ecclesia Christi**, together with Kleutgen's commentary.

The schema would have defined the infallibility of the Church as extending to "all those points which in matters of faith or morals are everywhere held or handed down as undoubted under bishops in communion with the Apostolic See, as well as all those points which are defined, either by those same bishops together with the Roman pontiff or by the Roman pontiff speaking *ex cathedra."* Kleutgen's commentary makes it clear that "morals" here refers to specific moral norms. Indeed, he argues at length that the Church can teach infallibly on new moral questions, with respect to which revelation says nothing implicitly or explicitly, because the answers to such questions are closely connected with revelation.

Having dealt with the position he rejects, Sullivan devotes the last section of his chapter on the infallibility of the ordinary magisterium to the opinion that no specific moral norm can be infallibly taught. He claims this is the view of "the majority of Catholic moral theologians today" and that "most of the Catholic theologians who have written on this question in recent years" subscribe to it. (149, 152). Thus, although he also summarizes some of the arguments offered for this view, Sullivan primarily relies on the authority of other theologians who hold it.

This appeal to the authority of other theologians is unsound in three ways. First, within theology, the weight of theological opinions is no greater than the evidence and arguments offered for them. Second, Sullivan begs the question by appealing to these opinions to complete his argument against us, for we have made our case against these same opinions. Third, the appearance of theological consensus in favor of the opinion Sullivan adopts is only that.

There are two substantial bodies of theological opinion. Which is the majority? Which is the minority? Who knows? Richard A. McCormick, S.J., writing in *Notes* 1984 (84) of those who support the Holy See's defense of Catholic teaching, says: "There are growing numbers of reactionary theologians who support this type of thing with insistence on a verbal conformity to the modern — and, I would add, open — mind." I dislike McCormick's adjectives, but am glad he sees the tide is turning.

According to Sullivan's summary, the "majority" view admits the possibility of infallible teaching concerning basic principles of natural law and of authoritative pastoral guidance on concrete problems. But it holds that specific norms of natural law "are neither formally nor virtually revealed" and that they cannot be deduced from revealed truths. The argument is that we arrive at concrete norms by shared reflection on experience; the process is inductive rather than deductive.

Sullivan adds that specific norms cannot be shown to be necessarily connected with revelation. Here the argument is based on the rule of Canon Law that nothing is to be considered infallibly defined or declared unless this is manifestly the case. Sullivan thinks this puts an impossible burden of proof on anyone who would try to show that a particular moral norm falls within the secondary object of infallibility (150).

In these arguments, Sullivan uses language which seems to narrow the class of moral norms which he claims cannot be infallibly taught. For instance, he says: "The concrete determinations of the natural law with regard to the complex problems facing people today are neither formally nor virtually revealed." Again, he refers to the "concrete and complex problems of modern man" (150). Such language might lead one to think of problems such as the morality of nuclear deterrence or *in vitro* fertilization.

However, granted (not conceded) that the solutions to such problems do not pertain to revelation, that does not entail that revelation neither contains nor implies any specific moral norm. Yet that is Sullivan's thesis. If it were not, one could grant his thesis but point out that contraception, adultery, abortion, and so on are not "complex problems of modern man," but fairly straightforward and perennial problems.

Sullivan's argument that specific moral norms cannot pertain to revelation if they depend upon shared reflection on experience not only assumes that all specific norms must be reached in this way, but that divine revelation can only be unfolded deductively. But that assumption would preclude the development of doctrine.

When Sullivan invokes the rule of Canon Law that nothing is to be considered infallibly defined or declared unless that is manifestly the case, he evidences a confusion, widespread among the theologians who share his view, between teaching infallibly proposed in solemn definitions and teaching infallibly proposed by the ordinary magisterium. For that rule of Canon Law refers to the former, not to the latter.

Sullivan ends the chapter by summarizing arguments for the thesis "that the concrete norms of the natural law simply do not admit of such irreversible determination" — that is, truth which would permanently preclude any need for substantial revision (151). The basic argument is one already used: that specific moral norms are reached by shared reflection upon experience. Sullivan thinks that passages in **Gaudium et spes**, 16, 33, and 46, which speak of searching for solutions to problems, support this thesis. He also says that the open-ended character of experience is such that moral absolutes are impossible: "We can never exclude the possibility that future experience, hitherto unimagined, might put a moral problem into a new frame of reference which would call for a revision of a norm that, when formulated, could not have taken such new experience into account." Finally, he invokes the opinion of Karl Rahner that the dynamism of human nature precludes specific moral norms with permanent validity (152).

The passages in **Gaudium et spes** which Sullivan cites clearly support the view that *some* moral questions call for shared reflection on experience, admit of no ready answers, and baffle everyone, including popes and other bishops. There are complex, fresh problems, such as how to order modern technology and industry to the common good, how to avoid the holocaust without surrendering to tyranny, and so forth. But **Gaudium et spes** makes it clear that there are at least some specific moral norms whose truth permanently precludes the possibility of substantial revision: for example, when it condemns genocide (GS 79). Obviously, genocide is a much greater immorality than contraception or adultery. However, the norm forbidding genocide is a specific moral norm. Indeed, this norm would not have been articulated without reflection upon some recent experience.

Again, the argument that the ongoing, open-ended character of experience precludes permanently true specific moral norms might be true with respect to *some* norms. But the argument only succeeds if someone establishes a theory of moral norms which shows the impossibility of moral absolutes. Many who deny moral absolutes think proportionalism is such a theory. However, there are strong reasons for considering proportionalism indefensible. In **The Way of the Lord Jesus**, Volume One, **Christian Moral Principles**, I state these reasons. There I also criticize Rahner's claim that the dynamism of human nature precludes specific moral norms with permanent validity (141-71; 859-60).

Vatican II's conditions for infallible teaching by the ordinary magisterium also include that the teaching be proposed *tamquam definitive tenendam* — as to be held definitively. Sullivan criticizes two of the four considerations Ford and I offer to show that this condition has been met in the case of the received teaching on contraception. To follow this argument, one must bear in mind a basic point: this requirement cannot mean that the infallible teaching of the ordinary magisterium must be expressed in the language of solemn definition. For the bishops dispersed throughout the world cannot define anything and do not use language of solemn definition in their day to day teaching.

Ford and I stated as follows what we think is meant by "as to be held definitively":

> The genesis of the text makes clear that what is demanded if the exercise of the ordinary magisterium is to be infallible is that a judgment be proposed for acceptance with an assent of certitude, similar to the assent of divine faith, but not necessarily having the same motive as has the latter assent. The formula in the second schema **De ecclesia Christi** of Vatican I, which Vatican II cites as comparable with its own teaching, refers to points held or handed down *as undoubted.* Thus, "to be held

definitively" clearly excludes cases in which a bishop proposes a view as a safe and probable opinion, but only as such.

A point of teaching surely is proposed as one to be held definitively if a bishop proposes it in the following way: not at his option but as part of his duty to hand on the teaching he has received; not as doubtful or even as very probable but as certainly true; and not as one which the faithful are free to accept or to reject but as one which every Catholic must accept.   (F-G, 275-76)

When Sullivan criticizes our arguments that the teaching on contraception has been proposed "as to be held definitively," he quotes the second paragraph of this explanation without the first, and then says: "Now it seems to me that there is a very real difference between authoritative teaching which calls upon the faithful to give their assent to it as certainly true, and the kind of teaching which proposes a doctrine as irreformably true and calls for an irrevocable assent" (146).

But, by "irreformably true" and "irrevocable assent," Sullivan sets a standard met only in the case of solemn definitions. In their day to day teaching, bishops do not individually propose doctrines as "irreformably true" and demand "irrevocable assent," even when they hand on revealed truths which call for the assent of faith. Rather, they simply teach truths — those which are revealed as such, those closely connected with revelation as certain, and those they consider sufficiently probable and important as safe judgments to accept and follow. Infallibility supervenes on acts of day to day teaching if all the conditions are met. But the bishops in teaching and the faithful in accepting their teaching usually do not reflect upon the supervening infallibility.

Ford and I offer four considerations to show that the teaching on contraception was proposed as a norm to be held definitively.

The second consideration we advance pivots on the fact that the teaching on contraception concerns grave matter. Sullivan call this our "principal argument" to show that the sinfulness of contraception was taught as a moral norm to be held definitively: "They base this claim primarily on the fact that the magisterium condemned contraceptive behavior as gravely sinful" (147).

Sullivan makes the point that a teaching could be proposed that something is gravely illicit without meaning that "the speculative question is definitively closed" (147). I concede this point and now say (contrary to Ford's and my summary of the argument): to propose a norm excluding some kind of act as mortally sinful need not be to propose a teaching to be held definitively. The content of the teaching and the kind of assent called for are at least logically distinct. A bishop could propose a norm excluding some kind of act (for example, working in an H-bomb factory) as mortally sinful but expressly propose that norm as probable rather than as certain. (But a conscientious bishop would not say *without qualification* that something is mortally sinful if he had the least doubt about it).

But while I concede that teaching about grave matter need not be proposed as to be held definitively, still I can complete the consideration Ford and I advanced by supplying a missing premise. We should have pointed out a norm for Catholic teachers on which St. Alphonsus and several other doctors of the Church insist: Catholic teachers never should unqualifiedly assert anything to be grave matter unless they are certain it is. This norm for pastors and teachers is almost always observed, because most try hard to avoid putting unnecessary burdens on the faithful. Hence, where grave matter is involved, the whole body of bishops in communion with the pope never will agree in unqualifiedly proposing a norm unless they consider it certain — to be held definitively.

Thus, I admit that there is no necessary logical relationship between the grave matter contained in a norm and the certain assent called for by those who teach it. But I deny that any sin was included all over the world in Christian lists of mortal sins unless the norm excluding that kind of act was received, held, and handed on as an inescapable requirement of God's plan for Christian life — not merely as "mortally certain" but as undoubted — to be held definitively.

Sullivan goes on further to the fourth consideration Ford and I advanced: "The other argument Ford and Grisez use to show that the doctrine on contraception was being taught as to be held definitively is that it was often proposed as a divinely revealed moral norm" (147). Sullivan's criticism of this argument is brief:

> Now it seems that if this argument were valid, it would eliminate practically all ordinary, non-definitive teaching by the magisterium. For whenever any appeal was made to Scripture in support of what was being taught, this would automatically become definitive teaching. Are we to conclude that the popes, who regularly appeal to Scripture in their encyclicals, have in all such cases been proposing their doctrine as definitively to be held? (148)

It seems to me this criticism involves two confusions. First, Sullivan here introduces the phrases "non-definitive teaching" and "definitive teaching." This language shifts the focus from the kind of assent called for to the teaching which calls for assent, and again suggests that the subject of discussion is teaching by solemn definitions. Actually, acceptance of Ford's and my argument would not "eliminate practically all ordinary, non-definitive teaching by the magisterium." It would merely mean that the part of this ordinary moral teaching which all the bishops in communion with the pope agree in proposing as certain has been taught infallibly — although lacking solemn definitions it is not "definitive teaching."

Second, the argument Ford and I make does not entail that whenever the popes appeal to Scripture in their encyclicals they are proposing their doctrine as to be held definitively. For instance, in **Humanae vitae** there are sixteen references to New Testament texts, but none of them is employed to found or support the central argument and conclusion. The same thing is true of most uses of Scripture in encyclicals.

But our detailed argument, which Sullivan ignores, Ford and I show that Scripture texts usually have been used precisely to found or support arguments for the conclusion that contraception is morally wrong. Today everyone is much more cautious than people once were about using proof texts, and Ford and I prescind from the question whether the use of Scripture texts to certify the teaching concerning contraception was sound. But we say that, when Catholic teachers claimed that God himself tells us that contraception is wrong, they proposed that norm as something divinely revealed, and thus called for an assent of faith. And that is the clearest way of proposing something *tamquam definitive tenendam.*

This consideration, it seems to me, is the decisive one. It explains why Christian teachers held not only this norm but other specific norms bearing on sex and innocent life, and proposed them to the faithful as obligatory standards for Christian living. They agreed in one judgment and proposed it so firmly because they held the common body of moral teaching, centering on and elaborating the Ten Commandments, with divine faith.

In a general audience on Wednesday, 18 July 1984, John Paul II reflected on the status and ground of the norm excluding contraception:

> The Church teaches this norm, although it is not formally (that is, literally) expressed in Sacred Scripture, and it does this in the conviction that the interpretation of the precepts of natural law belongs to the competence of the Magisterium.
>
> However, we can say more. Even if the moral law, formulated in this way in the Encyclical **Humanae Vitae**, is not found literally in Sacred Scripture, nonetheless, from the fact that it is contained in Tradition and — as Pope Paul VI writes — has been "very often expounded by the Magisterium" (**HV**, n. 12) to the faithful, it follows that this norm *is in accordance with the some total of revealed doctrine contained in biblical sources.*
>
> *(cf. **HV**, n. 4)*

The view that revelation includes no specific moral norms goes against the convictions of Christians down through the centuries. If one sets aside the twentieth century and considers the entire previous

Jewish and Christian tradition, its massiveness and unity are overwhelmingly impressive. For example, not only no Catholic but no other Christian and no Jew ever would have dared to say of adultery and killing the innocent anything but: these are wicked things, and they who do them, unless they repent, can have no part in God's kingdom. Contrary contemporary theological speculation has the burden of showing that even until yesterday the whole People of God grossly misunderstood His wise and loving commands.

Crisis in Religious Vocations

by

Fr. Thomas Dubay, S.M.

The title of the topic assigned to me this evening, "The Crisis in Religious Vocations," has an alarming ring to it in both meanings of that term. An alarm is in one sense a warning of danger, a summons to arms, and in another it is the noisy arousal from sleep. Those who love the Lord and take to heart the good of His people cannot fail to be alarmed about the sudden, precipitate and sharp decline in the numbers of young men and women entering religious life. While we may assume that many in the Church are indeed alarmed in the first sense, it seems safe to say that not a few need a crashing cymbal in the second sense. While we are dealing with a question to which pat and simplistic answers are commonly given, I shall attempt to be more thorough by breaking down our problem into four areas of concern:

1. Why in western technological societies has there been so sharp a decline in candidates for religious life?
2. Which religious institutes are attracting candidates and which are not?
3. What are the theological roots of this problem?
4. How ought we to promote vocations?

1. Why the sharp and sudden decline?

There are, I am convinced, approximately twenty reasons why American young men and women in frightening numbers are not responding to the radical call of the Gospel counsels. I shall sketch thirteen of them. Undoubtedly, God is calling many, but few are answering. Some of the reasons we religious can control, some we cannot. I shall begin with the latter.

First of all, young men and women are entangled in the increasing secularization of contemporary life together with the accompanying breakdown in moral probity: dishonesty, vanity, erotomania, money-centeredness, a fixation on sense pleasures and superficial amusements. All of this is an open contradiction to the hard road and the narrow gate that lead to life in any vocation.

Secondly, as a corollary of the first reason, we have the gradual but relentless breakdown in solid, faith-filled Catholic family life. Vocational responses through the centuries have abounded in homes blessed with prayerful, sainly parents. They have languished and continue to languish in worldly homes.

Thirdly, there is a wide-spread doubting of our Catholic faith. Agnosticism, even pious agnosticism, paralyzes any vibrant relationship with God. Skeptics do not lay down their lives for mere opinions, and to take the three evangelical counsels seriously is to lay down one's life. If this agnosticism were sealed away in academic towers, we would have less to concern us, but it is rampant. I think it is no exaggeration to say that millions of our young people are vocationally numbed by it. "Why should I give up what I can see, hear, touch, and feel," they wonder, "when priests and nuns themselves seem so confused, so disunited, so unsure? Why should I enter a vocation that thousands have been leaving?

A fourth obstacle is the public image of religious now fostered by the media. Talk shows, periodical articles, and stage plays do not feature the faithful, prayerful, obedient, happy priest and nun. Rather they love to present those least likely to attract healthy youth; namely, the bitter, the dissenting, the worldly, those unfaithful to their vows. This situation is one reason otherwise solid congregations sometimes do not attract many candidates: the public image is often so bad that the man on the street is likely to assume that all religious are probably like the ones he reads and hears about.

The fifth factor is the alarming increase in psychological woundedness and chemical dependency amoung our youth and their parents. We are seeing an increasing number of applicants who, good as their intentions may be, could not possibly live a peaceful, happy, productive community life whether in marriage or in the convent. In many cases it is by no means clear that therapy would make them fit.

A sixth reason is the pervasive relativism of our day: the slow but relentless shift in recent decades from the objective mind to the subjective mind; that is, from the conviction of absolute truth in morals and religion to the relativistic persuasion that anything is acceptable if, as the saying goes, it turns you on. Thus, just as one accepts or rejects theism, the divinity of Christ, the claims of the Catholic Church, not after careful study of objective evidence but according to one's felt likes and dislikes, so also one embraces marriage or priesthood or religious life (or makes no commitment to anything) not after a prayerful consideration of the divine will, but merely according to one's feelings.

While the six problems we have just sketched lie beyond the

control of religious, those to which we now turn our attention do fall under this control, at least to some extent. Hence, element number seven: there is a sharp decline in Catholic school enrollment together with an erosion in the content of religion courses in the schools we still do operate. Youngsters who are not sure of the divinity of Christ, who have no clear picture of the divinely founded Church, who are encouraged to form their own moral opinions by mere value clarification, are hardly going to be attracted to the Gospel counsels of which they know nothing at all.

An eighth factor is the lack of promotion of vocations or even an opposition to them by parents, priests, and religious. At the one extreme are those who do not encourage the young to give their lives to God through the vows because they themselves do not believe in that life or even, at times, in the Church herself. On the other extreme are those sincere priests and religious who cannot identify with the secularization of their own institutes, and who cannot therefore in conscience advise youth to enter them.

A ninth obstacle, which we religious can control, is the fire or the lack of fire that characterizes our lives. Plain honesty requires that we admit to a great deal of contemporary laxity among far too many of us: little prayer and less poverty, extensive wardrobes and elegant dining, worldly amusements and expensive vacations, frequent pleasure trips, including overseas excursions. Affluent upper middle class living is not attractive to young men and women already disillusioned with materialism, already touched by grace to seek the things above, already beginning to fall in love with God. They may not yet be saints, but they are not stupid. They are repelled by religious who claim to be poor with the poor Christ and yet are dressed in fine clothes, and who eat, drink, and recreate in manners indistinguishable from lay people in the $40,000 wage bracket.

Perhaps, I should be a trifle blunt: many of us, lay and religious alike, are no longer in love with God. Some of us are so spent and jaded by the tinsel of the world that we fail even to see the unspeakable glory of the Incarnate Word — some may not even know what this last sentence means. We are little interested in being poor with the poor Christ, in being obedient to the very death with him, in living chastely in an erotically sated generation. Not being passionately in love with uncreated Beauty, we have no depth in our prayer life. Having still some remnants of goodness in us, we therefore spill ourselves out in secondary good things and leave on the periphery the primary. We get absorbed in politics and sociology and a whole list of -isms. Some go so far as to reject the Church because she refuses to adopt their agenda, an agenda which has little to distinguish it from the agenda of the world. It should surprise no one that youth who want God are not drawn by what they see in us.

The increasing invisibility of priests and religious is our tenth problem. Whether an organization is selling cars or recruiting personnel, the advertising programs heavily depend on the visual attraction of persons and pictures. If people seldom saw what a Pontiac looks like, few Pontiacs would be sold. If Marines had no distinguishable dress and even less esprit de corps, I cannot imagine youth being in the least interested in them. Today one rarely sees a priest or a sister on the street. They are now seldom seen in airports, whereas formerly one saw them often. Another sign of transcendence has disappeared.

The eleventh factor is stark: Jesus is not known as He really is. No person in his right mind will consent to give up marriage, to be poor in fact, to obey other human beings he need not obey, unless he falls in love. *The* reason for embracing religious life is not merely to get a job done, not even an excellent job. *The* reason is the towering figure of the Lord Jesus. His sheer originality, unique beauty, complete uninventability, and overwhelming light will draw men and women to a genuine vocation as nothing else will.[1] We need to teach Him, yes, but we must also live Him. Young men and women need to see in religious and priests a touch of transcendence, a luminous love, a radiant joy such as can derive only from the Crucified-risen One. Lest you think I am rhapsodizing, let me speak a moment of Father Michael Tansi, a Nigerian priest of our own century, a priest whose life reminds one of the Cure of Ars. Over one-half of the priests of his diocese came from his parish.[2] To get the feel for this astonishing phenomenon, suppose that in an American diocese of 400 priests about 210 of them came from one parish. You would conclude that something is happening in that parish, and you would be right. What is happening is sanctity. One of Father Tansi's proteges, later recalling his vocation, wrote of the impression his pastor made on him as a boy: "You knew he was near God, not just a priest having a name ... After I saw him, I said I wanted to be like him. Nobody preached to us to be a priest. It was just seeing him."[3] Father Tansi presented to his parishoners what the Lord Jesus looked like, and they liked what they saw. The young came and they stayed.

The twelfth element in our situation is a simple lack of general instruction in the theology behind the three evangelical counsels. St. Ambrose in the 4th century presented from his pulpit an account of consecrated virginity so powerful, so attractive, so compelling, that mothers would keep their daughters away from his sermons, for young women were embracing the virginal life in droves. I do not recall once in my life hearing from a parish pulpit on Sunday morning a coherent account of why a young man or woman should want to be poor and celibate with the poor and celibate Christ. Yes, I have heard pleas for vocations, but never were they more than superficial exhortations based on apostolic needs. In our high schools today, several weeks may be devoted to an explanation of the sacrament of matrimony in senior high religion class, but to my knowledge not one day is devoted to an explanation of consecrated virginity. The eloquence, fire, and depth of Bishop Ambrose as he expounded this way of life so successfully seem in short supply today among his successors in the episcopal and sacerdotal ministries.

Finally, there is the radical problem that cuts across and through all our other problems; namely, original sin and our own selfishness. There can be no doubt that God amply gives the call to the three counsels according to his goodness and the needs of the Church — to suppose otherwise would be to question providence. And few would doubt that the Church today is in dire need of an abundance of authentic religious men and women. Hans Urs von Balthasar is quite right in my judgment in saying that the Holy Spirit calls many more youths to the evangelical counsels than most of us suspect.[4] But how many of these youths give the call deliberate, prayerful, serious consideration for five minutes in a row? God forces no one. He alone knows how many of our youth say an indirect "no" as they prefer to pursue the slick glitter, the deadening permissiveness, the sterile vanity, the illusory sensuality of the beckoning world. Insofar as you and I have not shown them in life and word the saints' answers to all this, we are at fault. But they, too, are responsible for their free choices. Yes, plain sin is a large part of the vocation problem, and almost no one dares to say it.

2. Which institutes are attracting vocations and which are not?

Now that we have partially explained why there has been a drastic reduction in candidates for religious life, we may turn our attention to a related question. What kind of institute is attracting the young who do enter and faithfully remain, and what kind attracts few or none? As I work both in our own country and abroad, I find the evidence overwhelming. Some congregations are attracting very large numbers. As of this writing, the Missionaries of Charity has over 400 novices with 80 Americans in their formation program. The Carmelite Sisters of the Sacred Heart has 135 professed, with 11 novices and 8 postulants. The Daughters of St. Paul has 150 professed in the United States, 25 novices and 40 postulants. The Immaculate Heart of Mary Sisters in Nigeria has 352 professed, 81 novices and 179 postulants. The Oblates of the Virgin Mary has 135 priests and 20 brothers in the entire world and they have over 200 students studying for the priesthood. Of this number 75 are

Americans. These are publicly known facts, and they do not need further documentation here. What does need to be noted, indeed to be proclaimed, are the striking differences between institutes like these which do and others which do not attract the young. I shall summarize these differences under several captions.

1. **Lifestyle** Young people are choosing communities that put prayer first, live a genuine frugality, believe in obedience, and, therefore, have not abandoned the essentials of the religious life. They are avoiding groups that have conceived of renewal as a stripping down operation, a gradual abandonment of one obligation after another, always, of course, in the name of updating. Institutes that have neglected or rejected the essentials, that have embraced a whole series of mitigations, whose lifestyle is anything but prophetic, have empty novitiates.

2. **Unity** Successful institutes are united, while the dying ones are polarized. Congregations whose main thrust has been toward secularization invariably have, in my experience, a large minority who reject what has been imposed upon them. They are sharply divided, a fact that is apparent to anyone who has grassroots contacts with them. Their polarization bespeaks uncertainty, confusion, and even conflict. They are not corporately attractive.

3. **Visible Witness** Most young men and women are drawn to communities that have retained a religious habit, while they avoid those which have embraced secular dress. Every institute I know of which is attracting large numbers of candidates has a uniform garb.

4. **Ecclesial obedience** Institutes which are gladly receptive of Catholic teaching and discipline are prospering, while those whose leadership reject this teaching and discipline are withering on the vine. The evidence is striking and, indeed, unmistakable. It is not only that God rewards obedience with His blessing: it is also the simple fact that authenticity works.

5. **Theological validity** We may summarize the difference between vibrant communities and those in a moribund condition by saying that the former are following the only viable theology of the three counsels that we have, while the latter have no coherent theology at all. Secularized institutes are following a curious and selective admixture of some favored Gospel ideas together with what they call their "lived experiences." The latter are sometimes at odds both with Scripture and with canon law.

6. **Vocation vs. career** Young men and women are seeking admittance into communities which are pursuing a vocation; they are avoiding those which seem to be following careers. The life of the counsels is not

a job to be done (i.e., a career). It is participation in the paschal mystery, a particular way of being in love with God — i.e., it is a vocation. Youth may not know the theory behind this distinction, but they do have the acumen to grasp that men and women whose predominant concern is work to be done are not pursuing a vocation.

3. What are the theological roots of this problem?

We turn next to the core of our concern, the center from which the ramifications radiate. Because a call to the evangelical counsels originates in the trinitarian life and thus is a supernatural, not a mere sociological reality, it is not surprising that the heart of our problem lies in a misconstruing of its theological roots. Those religious who see themselves as pursuing a career, a job to be done before all else, have embraced a lifestyle that is more or less atheological according as they relegate prayer more or less to the periphery. Being out of touch with the sources of revelation, not to mention canon law, it is not a cause of wonder that, when they seek candidates, they propose the unrealistic pictures we see in their advertising and in their brochures and self-descriptions. To make this point clear, I must summarize what the New Testament says about consecrated chastity.

Virginity/celibacy in the Gospel is a privileged sphere of the sacred. Chapter 19 of Matthew presents continence for the kingdom as related to humility and poverty in creating an inner emptiness which sensitizes one to the movings of the Holy Spirit. This vast void bestows on the person who embraces it with and for the Lord Jesus a radical readiness for what He means and what He is about. Neither Jesus nor Paul mention work to be done when they speak about celibacy for the kingdom (Mt. 19: 12; 1 Cor. 7:32-35).[5] What they do proclaim is that celibacy puts one on the same wave length as the celibate lord who is exclusively concerned with the Father's will and with nothing else (Jn. 4:34). The virgin is totally wrapped up in the Lord, says Paul, and in no one else. This is why complete chastity for the kingdom deepens the baptismal consecration: it is a more radical pursuit of God, a more direct seeking of the things above (Col. 3:1-2).

Secondly, virginity in the New Testament is a spousal focusing on the Lord with undivided attention. It is a being-in-love matter before it is anything else. Celibacy for the kingdom is an intense, total living of what the Church is; namely, as St. Paul puts it, "a virgin married to Christ" (2 Cor. 11:2). Once again, therefore, we are dealing with a vocation, not with an employment.

Thirdly, virginity is the fulfillment vocation par excellence. True it is that every vocation lived according to the divine plan fulfills; but this one, being an exclusive, direct-path pursuit of the divine fullness, is more efficient in bringing about the new creation. This is the point Jesus makes when He declares that those who give up property and marriage for the kingdom get "much more in the present time" as well as eternal life (Lk. 18:29-30). One could not rightly give up the great good of wedded love and parenthood except for a still greater love and parenthood. As Canon 1191, #1 points out, no one can take a vow except for some greater good.

Let me make the point in still another manner. Suppose I were invited to speak on religious life to 300 seniors in one of our high schools, and suppose I were limited to 50 minutes. In terms teenagers would grasp, I would begin by explaining what may be called existential boredom — that is, boredom not with this particular book or party or date or lecture, but boredom with life in general. This explanation would take perhaps five minutes. Then I would say, "You know, there is only one kind of being in visible creation that is capable of existential boredom — namely, a human being." It would take another five or ten minutes to explain why one must have an intellect to be bored. Then we would proceed to notice that this is why only the infinite can fill a human person, and why immersion in God ("We call it contemplation," I'd add) is the sole answer to the human puzzle. This would take another ten minutes. Only with this background would we be ready to talk about the vows as they really are. There is one vocation, I would continue, whose main purpose is this deep immersion in God — the lifestyle is tailor-made to make this immersion easier to attain. Then I would unfold a bit of what we considered a few minutes ago about consecrated virginity in the New Testament. All this would take about 20 minutes. Finally, I would add a word about the secondary purpose of religious life, the external apostolates some institutes also pursue.

There are several advantages in this approach to promoting vocations. One is that it is real: this is the way religious life actually exists in the Christic economy. Good theology makes good practice. A second advantage is that the students would find the talk interesting, even absorbing. This I know from experience, for I have spoken about existential boredom to teenagers, and their ears perk up at the very mention of it. They know what I am talking about, for they have experienced it in themselves and/or in their friends. A third advantage is that this approach begins where the students are, not where we might like them to be. Any effective teacher puts himself in the minds of his listeners — he begins where they are. One reason the usual vocation talk falls on deaf ears is that the students do not have the background to appreciate what is said even when what is said is correct. A fourth advantage is that this explanation makes sense to anyone in any vocation. If one grants that God is the sole answer to the human puzzle, a way of life that focuses on Him as its primary thrust makes immense sense. For the first time in their lives these young people would see the point of making vows of chastity, poverty, and obedience. A fifth advantage is that the majority of the 300 seniors who will enter marriage may later in 15 or 20 years avoid opposing a vocation in a son or daughter because they once heard an explanation that was coherent and consistent with a vibrant theism.

One of the most distressing elements in our vocational picture today is the alarming shallowness of the analyses offered by men and women at the administrative level of vocation organizations in the United States. For example, a vocations report recently made by an official of the United States Catholic Conference "cited celibacy, the permanent commitment, and lack of encouragement from parents and priests as the main reason for the drop in vocations." [7] Another sacerdotal official, the Executive Director of Vocations of the USSC, said that the "real problem is the multitude of options that face young people today." A sister member of the administrative board of the National Catholic Vocation Council is cited in the same article as saying that vocation is coming to mean "professional Church service." [8] It must be noted that of the five reasons given in these statements two indicate the problem to be the charism of celibacy and its permanency, one a lack of encouragement, and two the problem of religious life as a career.

Let me comment briefly on each of these official explanations. To consider permanent celibacy as a problem to one who has the gift is like calling grace a problem. The problem lies not in the charism but in the one who rejects it or refuses to live according to it. The Holy Spirit, giver of all gifts, is not a problem. The third explanation, lack of encouragement, has some validity (as we have noted), but, mentioned by itself, it is shallow. What needs to be explained is why priests and parents fail to encourage young people — the answer to this question returns us to the first section of our paper. The "options" and "professional Church service" explanations are simply bad theology or no theology at all: they make celibate consecration a mere career.

It is distressing that these publicly-cited official explanations fail to mention the obvious and multiple reasons we have already dealt with in the first section of our discussion. The official views are un-self-critical. They suppose that there is really nothing wrong with the way many priests, sisters, and brothers are living their lives, for they say not a word about defects. They seem unaware likewise of what young people think of the secularized version of religious life. As one young woman recently said of herself as she began to seek out and visit various communities, hoping to enter one of them: "I had no idea of what had taken place in communities after Vatican II ..... (but) I knew what I *didn't* want as soon as I saw it." [9]

Disturbing, too, is the omission in these official explanations of any reference to the most striking evidence available even to uneducated people — namely, the sharp differences between liberalizing institutes which attract few or none and the faithful ones which attract many. That a national task force on vocations is going to advise our bishops' committee on vocations on the basis of this sort of analysis is frightening.[10] If we do not acknowledge the illness, how can we apply the remedy?

A final note. The whys and wherefores of the vocation crisis are not obscure, mysterious, or arcane. What is mysterious, what does surprise a careful observer, what does need explanation, is how and why so many people do not see the overwhelming evidence that is clear to so many others. It is doubtlessly significant that those who do see the analysis are precisely the members of those institutes which are attracting young men and women, often in very large numbers, whereas those who seem not to see are the leaders of those institutes which are attracting few or none. I can only say that reality has its revenge on those who deny it. Reality has the last word.

FOOTNOTES

[1] See Hans Urs von Balthasar, **The Glory of the Lord,** vol. 1, p. 177.

[2] **Cistercian Studies,** 1981, p. 489.

[3] **Ibid.**

[4] Hans Urs von Balthasar, **The Christian State of Life,** pp. 465-468.

[5] See also Lucien Legrand, **The Biblical Doctrine of Virginity.**

[6] *National Catholic Reporter,* April 15, 1983, p. 11.

[6] The official is Father Eugene Hemrick and the quotation comes from the *National Catholic Register,* November 4, 1984, p. 2.

[8] **Ibid.**, September 19, 1982, p. 1.

[9] Sister Juliana Bernice Wollack, D.S.P., "Youth Seek Sacrifice-Holiness," *Religious Life,* November, 1984, p. 3.

[10] See *The Catholic Herald,* Superior, WI, November 1, 1984, p. 7.

Derrida or Deity?
Deconstruction in the Presence of the Word

by

R. V. Young

Recently I was teaching a course in the "Classical Backgrounds of English Literature." During one class I was attempting to explain how Virgil had established in the Dido episode of the **Aeneid** a thematic complex which had reverberated throughout the development of Western literature in a series of binary oppositions of which one term was always the focus of moral superiority: honor vs. love, duty vs. pleasure, public office vs. private inclination. As I pointed out how Aeneas' epic heroism was virtually defined by his self-denying role in the fulfillment of destiny, one of my students objected. A very shrewd young lady, she argued that the **Aeneid** could be read in preciselly the opposite fashion, that — given Aeneas' unrelenting anguish, his reluctance to struggle or inflict pain, only gradually overcome as he hardens into the ruthless butcher of Turnus at the close of the poem — given these features, Virgil could be seen as a covert sympathizer with Dido, pacificism, and the rejection of the imperial destiny associated with the Olympian gods. "It sounds like you're trying to do a deconstructive reading," I remarked, and immediately regretted it. But it was too late; the word had already slipped out. "I've heard so much about *deconstruction* lately," another student said. "Could you *deconstruct* the **Aeneid** for us?"

I looked at my watch and demurred; I did not think the job could be managed in the fifteen minutes remaining in that class. Still, now that deconstruction has become of concern even to undergraduates, and seems even to have filtered into their view of literary works, it will not be amiss for us to take stock of its relationship to Catholic intellectual life. At the heart of the controversy in this country stands the English department of Yale University, or, at least, its "Hermeneutical Mafia," comprising Harold Bloom, Geoffrey Hartman, J. Hillis Miller, and the late Paul deMan. These four stand accused of subverting objective standards of literary interpretation, of blurring the distinction between criticism and imaginative literature, of deprecating the author and authorial intention for the sake of the imaginative gambits of the critical interpreter, and of engaging in a generally self-indulgent, irresponsible style of writing, which undercuts the scholarly and educational aims of academic discourse. The evidence for these indictments was not gathered by FBI wiretap; it is readily available in published sources. "Criticism is . . . continuous with the language of literature," writes J. Hillis Miller, one of the more vociferous of the *mafiosi*. And he continues in this vein:

> The poem [Shelley's *Triumph of Life*$_1$], like all texts, is "unreadable," if by "readable" one means a single, definitive interpretation. In fact, neither the "obvious" reading nor the "deconstructionist" reading is "univocal." Each contains, necessarily, its enemy within itself, is itself both host and parasite. The deconstructionist reading contains the obvious one and vice versa. Nihilism is an unalienable alien presence within Occidental metaphysics, both in poems and in the criticism of poems.[1]

It is apparent that more is involved here than an altercation among English teachers over passing literary fashion. Critical theory is necessarily inscribed within metaphysics, and, as the quotation from Hillis Miller makes explicit, the deconstructionists are especially aggressive in collapsing the partitions, not only between literature and criticism, but among all forms of discourse. There is more at stake in deconstruction than a new reading of **Bleak House** or William Blake. Not only the possibility of meaning, but the status of being itself is put in question. This is not surprising, since lurking behind the attack on conventional literary interpretation mounted by Yale's "Gang of Four" is the somewhat sinister figure of the French philosopher, Jacques Derrida.

It is Derrida who seems to have coined the term "deconstruction," by which he means not only a method of radical textual analysis, but a whole new way of thinking about the human experience of reality. What is, finally, to be deconstructed is the whole "logocentric" tradition of Western metaphysics, or "ontotheology" as Derrida often calls it. From a Derridean perspective, reality itself — or at least mankind's apprehension of it — is a kind of writing; and deconstruction seizes on the loose linguistic threads to unravel the textuality of the world. Derrida thus threatens the the intellectual norms of Western culture. Yet deconstruction is not wholly a cause for alarm. It is a corrosive solvent to the utopian pieties of secular humanism and Marxism, but the Catholic faith remains basically untouched, although it is the ultimate "ontotheology" or "philosophy of presence." While the Derridean abyss opens sickeningly at the feet of contemporary humanism, it offers little terror to Catholics, whose saints have plumbed its depths in centuries past. The crucial "innovations" of deconstruction have been already perceived and assimilated by the doctors of the Church.

Born of Sephardic Jewish parents in Algiers in 1930, Jacques Derrida is professor of philosophy at the Ecole Normale Superieure in

Paris, a position he has held for more than a decade balanced with regular visiting professorships in the United States, first at Johns Hopkins and now at Yale. He drew broad attention in this country in 1966 with a paper delivered at an international symposium at Johns Hopkins. Derrida's paper, entitled "Structure, Sign, and Play in the Discourse of the Human Sciences," was basically a critique of the structuralism of Claude Levi-Strauss just when structuralism was at its highest prestige. The following year saw the publication of no fewer than three books by Derrida: **Speech and Phenomena,** a critique of Husserl's theory of signs; **Writing and Difference,** a collection of essays; and **Of Grammatology,** a critique of the Western world's traditional privileging of actual speech over writing. In 1972, three more volumes from Derrida appeared: **Disseminations, Margins,** and **Positions,** the last a collection of interviews. Although at least three more volumes have appeared since, these are certainly the most influential and important.[2]

A useful perspective on deconstruction is secured by approaching it as the ingrate stepchild of Parisian structuralism, an academic movement which sought to place the human sciences on the same epistemological footing as the physical sciences. The principal intellectual inspiration for structuralism lies in the work of Marx and Freud, who both sought to analyze human behavior in terms of objectively conceived economic or psychological structures without worrying about the messy, unscientific business of the conscious individual will. The methodological model for structuralism, however, came from linguistics, most notably the **Course in General Linguistics,** posthumously compiled from lecture notes by students of Ferdinand de Saussure. Hence leading structuralists are usually linguists (like Roman Jacobson), or those who apply the structural model of linguistics to other disciplines such as psychology (like Jacques Lacan) or anthropology (like Claude Levi-Strauss).

It has been widely noted that Derrida's great perception is that the basic principle of Saussurian structural linguistics — "That no intrinsic relationship obtains between the two parts of the sign, signifier, and signified" — undercuts even the structuralist enterprise itself. A signifier, or sound-image, Saussure maintains, is arbitrarily linked to a signified, or concept; that is, since the sounds of words, or signifiers, are unmotivated conventions, a sign is a structure of difference: "The important thing in the word is not the sound alone but the phonic differences that make it possible to distinguish this word from all others, for differences carry signification."[3] This means that *all* discourse is subject to the same leakage of meaning precisely in order to mean at all. The very act of meaning — that is, of signifying — implies the absence of the signified which, therefore, can be grasped not in itself but only by means of the substituted signifier. hence we confront not merely the gap between *res* and *verbum,* but a gap, or *aporia,* within the sign itself, which, in Saussure's terminology, is the complex of signifier and signified. Hence, the structuralist himself can never stand outside the structures he posits; he, too, is an inmate of the "prison house of language." [4]

Now for Derrida this principle of linguistics and semiotics has important metaphysical — I should say *anti-metaphysical* — implications. Since man inhabits a universe of discourse, he is entangled in a chain of signifiers referring to absent signifieds: the world is thus one great circular definition. Every human term or concept is marked by what Derrida calls the *trace* of its incompletion and undecidability, and this applies with full force to subjective consciousness. In his earliest published works he attacks the notion of the self-possessed intentional subject of Husserlian phenomenology. There is no prelinguistic thought, Derrida maintains, fully present to the transcendental consciousness: "As soon as we admit this continuity of the now and the not-now, perception and non-perception, in the zone of primordiality common to primordial impression and primordial retention, we admit the other into the self-identity of the *Augenblick;* nonpresence and nonevidence are admitted into the *blink of an instant.* There is duration to the blink, and it closes the eye." [5] This means that our knowledge, deployed in temporally extended signifiers, cannot all be simultaneously present. We know only in memory or in expectation; hence we know only what is not here and now, not present.

Our world of consciousness is not, then, inhabited by the presentation of its intentional objects, but by *re-presentations* implicated with *differance.* This neologism, spelled with an "a" rather than an "e" in the last syllable, is derived from the French verb *differer,* which, like its Latin cognate, *differre,* means both to defer in time or postpone, and to differ or be spatially distinct. The world "child," for example, is a "sound-image" which signifies a complex, equivocal notion: offspring, non-adult, immature person, innocent or inexperienced person, and so on. But then all of these terms, these "signifieds," also turn out to be signifiers which likewise ramify into another set of signifieds which spawn more signifiers. There can be no end to this process, no final, central concept or signified which can logically or fully account for the meanings which float freely around the arbitrary sound-image "child." *A fortiori* no particular visual image in the mind or in actual reality (i.e., a specific, individual child) can exhaust the implications of the term. "Child" has meaning *only* because it is distinguishable from other sound-images ("man," "adult," "baby," "parent"), *not* because it is rooted in a stable signification.

Derrida thus seems to have gone a step beyond nominalism; he seems to suggest that substance occurs in a matrix of accidents, and he calls the latter *differance*.

Differance is, then, the defect or incompletion inscribed not only in every human utterance, but also in every human experience; the *trace* is the token, silent and invisible — literally nonexistent — of this interval or gap in being. Because writing is so plainly representational, a supplement for speech, it manifests the "textuality" of human experience. Hence, it is characteristically repressed in favor of the spoken word, with its illusion of unmediated presence by the Western metaphysical tradition which ceaselessly strives to occupy the vacancy in human experience, to fill the hole in being:

> The subordination of the trace to the full presence summed up in the logos, the humbling of writing beneath a speech by an onto-theology determining the archeological and eschatological meaning of being as presence, as parousia, as life without differance: another name for death, historical metonymy where God's name holds death in check. That is why, if this movement begins its era in the form of Platonism, it ends in infinitist metaphysics. Only infinite being can reduce the difference in presence. In that sense, the name of God, at least as it is pronounced within classical rationalism, is the name of indifference itself.[6]

For all the evident radicalism and anti-theism of such comments, Derrida's deconstruction of Western metaphysics has increasingly proven a source of unease to Marxist critics in recent years. Hence Edward W. Said, Columbia University's resident Palestinian anti-imperialist, is dubious about Derrida's ideological commitment:

> If everything in a text is always open equally to suspicion and to affirmation, then the differences between one class interest and another, between oppressor and oppressed, one discourse and another, one ideology and another, are virtual in — but never crucial to making decisions about — the finally reconciling element of textuality.[7]

The explicit charge here is that Derrida is unwilling to get his hands dirty in history and radical politics. Frank Lentricchia, another literary critical fellow traveler, complains: "Derrida's deconstructive project is formalist through and through."[8] It is hard to conceive a more damning term in the current critical lexicon than "formalist." But the real worry is that Marx is quite as vulnerable to deconstruction — really more so — than Plato or Hegel. "A speech dreaming its plenitude" is a perfect description of the discourse of the radical left, with its binary oppositions of class conflict and its "eschatological" project of full human "presence" in a classless society devoid of repression. Deconstructed Marxism turns out to be secularized millenarianism, a self-deceived, materialist logocentrism. In this sense, the logic of Derrida's deconstruction is reminiscent of

Jacques Monod, who quite openly dismissed Marxism as simply the last in a long line of "animist" myths seeking a center of originary meaning inscribed in the meaninglessness of the physical universe.[9]

But what, then, of Christianity and the deconstructive project? Most of Derrida's impact — his shock value — arises from his demonstration that supposedly "critical" philosophies, exemplars of post-Enlightenment thought, are covertly logocentric; that is, that they are founded on the absolutizing of human reason or consciousness even as they claim to liberate us from divine absolutes. As the force of God's presence is diminished, the autonomous human subject becomes "transcendental signified" of its own signification. But Christianity has always been explicitly "logocentric"; paradoxically, its confrontation with God — the radically other for which every sign is inadequate — has forced Christian theology to deal with the issues Derrida raises, although in different terms, from the first. In this connection it is interesting that Derrida, so far as I know, has not discussed St. Augustine and St. Thomas Aquinas. He would have to acknowledge that in their work the human condition had already been radically "deconstructed." And what is a man, any man," Augustine questions, "when only a man?" [10]

In the **Confessions** Augustine's preoccupation with time and memory anticipates Derrida's notion of *differance*. Augustine recognizes that even as we cannot grasp the present moment in our temporal existence in the physical world, even so our speech is never wholly and immediately present. But Augustine also maintains that these limitations are also the conditions of being, action, and knowledge. In order for discrete substances — beings distinct from necessary Being — to exist at all, they must suffer displacement in time, and the same temporal displacement is requisite for the differential process of speech:

> So much you gave to these things, because they are parts of a whole, which do not all exist at the same time, but all function in the universe, of which they are parts, succeeding one another and then giving way. Notice how our speech operates in the same way by means of signifying sounds. For an utterance is not complete, if one word does not give way, when its syllables have sounded, so that another can succeed it.[11]

Augustine perceives that in its very temporal progression, speech lacks complete reality, and, in this, it faithfully mirrors the incompleteness of human — indeed, of all temporal existence. But the discontinuities of spatio-temporal existence are not an insufficiency of being as such. The very incompleteness of being as it unfolds in time and space entails an absolute Being as its ground; the stream of our words into the abyss of oblivion — of signifiers pursuing elusive signifieds — entails the being of the immutable Word of God:

> And what was being spoken is not ended, and something else spoken, so
> that everything might be said, but everything is said at the same time and
> eternally; otherwise there would be time and change, and no true eternity
> or immortality.[12]

Differance, Derrida maintains, inhabits the existential gaps of time:
"nonpresence and nonevidence are admitted into the *blink of an instant,*"
the blink which "closes the eye." [13] But this is merely a human perspective. St. Augustine might reply that God does not blink; His eye never
closes.

Derrida of course demurs; he dismisses even "the most negative
order of negative theology" as dependent upon the prior trace of *differance,* which "has neither existence nor essence," which "belongs to no
category of being, present or absent." Like the lines which define plane
surfaces in geometry while having no breadth themselves, *differance* is
the negative prerequisite of any apprehension of being:

> Not only is *differance* irreducible to every ontological or theological —
> onto-theological — reappropriation, but it opens up the very space in
> which onto-theology — philosophy — produces its system and its history.
> It thus encompasses and irrevocably surpasses onto-theology or phi-
> losophy.[14]

But if *differance* is the all-encompassing ground of being, then this
ground is a hole, an abyss, and being itself becomes problematic, endlessly "deferred:"

> "Older" than Being itself, our language has no name for such a *differance.*
> But we "already know" that if it is unnamable, this is not simply provisional;
> it is not because our language has still not found or received this *name,*
> or because we would have to look for it in another language, outside the
> finite system of our language. It is because there is no *name* for this, not
> even essence or Being — not even the name "difference," which is not
> a name, which is not a pure nominal unity, and continually breaks up in a
> chain of different substitutions.[15]

"What is unnamable," Derrida continues, "is not some ineffable being" —
God, for instance — but "the play that brings about nominal effects."
Hence there is no "unique word," no "master name," nothing "keryg-
matic" about the "word" with a lower case "w." [16]

Now Derrida's reduction of metaphysics to a *Mise en Abime* rests
in his perception of the spatiotemporal dislocation of human perception
and signification. Our saying and knowing are attenuated and fragment-
ed in time and space, which in Derridean deconstruction, as in Einstein-
ian relativity, tend to converge. *To be in time,* Derrida urges, is a contradiction because movement in time entails continuous loss of presence:
"The present alone is and ever will be. Being is presence or the modifica-

tion of presence." [17] Hence even the assertion of the contrary deconstructs itself as it unfolds as temporal speech:

> The *I am*, being experienced only as an *I am present*, itself presupposes the relationship with presence in general, with being as presence. The appearing of the *I* to itself in the *I am* is thus originally a relation with its own possible disappearance. Therefore, *I am* originally means *I am mortal*. *I am immortal* is an impossible proposition. We can even go further: as a linguistic statement "I am he who am" is the admission of a mortal. [18]

Derrida's appraisal of the paradox of temporal being is by no means novel; St. Augustine grapples with it at great length in the **Confessions** and reaches virtually the same impasse regarding being in time:

> How therefore do two of these times, past and present, exist, when the past already is not, and the future is not yet? As for the present, if it were always present and did not move into the past, it would not be time but rather eternity. If then the present comes to be time only because it moves into the past, how can we say *it is*, when the cause of its being is that it will not be; in fact how can we say truly that time is, except insofar as it tends not to be? [19]

What distinguishes this passage from Derrida's disquisition on "temporalization" is that Augustine invokes the concept of eternity which Derrida steadfastly ignores. The lurking (non)presence of the trace, of *differance* — the fissure in being — undermines the possibility of *simplicity*, which is a necessary attribute of Eternity, of God. But this view fails to take into account Derrida's own insights regarding the fallibility of man's knowledge. "There has never been any 'perception,' " Derrida writes, "contrary to what our desire cannot fail to be tempted into believing, the thing itself always escapes." [20] But what "always escapes" cannot be confidently relegated to nonexistence. Derrida succeeds in refuting the transcendental aspirations of man *qua* man as temporal creature, but he says nothing to disprove an eternity which transcends the temporal limitations which bound us. Indeed if the "thing" always "escapes" us, then there must be a something which escapes. The very notion of being wrong entails something to be wrong about.

St. Augustine points out that the inherent fallibility of our perception requires that we try to conceive the basis of true perception on a wholly other mode. Even if we could imagine a mind that knew the entire history of the world, past and future, as well as might know a familiar psalm, remembering what was sung, anticipating what remained — such a mind would still be incommensurably inferior to God's. Even a mind with a hypothetically infinite memory and foreknowledge would still be bound by time. We must, Augustine urges, think of God's knowledge in completely different terms:

> Your knowledge is far, far more wonderful and far more mysterious. It

does not come to you as a well-known psalm to the singer or hearer, whose emotions are changed and senses divided with the expectation of words to come and the memory of those gone by. You are unalterably eternal; that is, the truly eternal creator of minds. Therefore just as you knew *heaven and earth in the beginning* without any change in your knowledge, even so you made *heaven and earth in the beginning* without any expansion of your activity. Let him who understands praise you; let him who understands not praise you.[21]

Derrida successfully shows that logocentric self-identity is a contradiction for a being in the temporal mode such as man, even for such a being with infinite capacities. But as St. Augustine's discussion shows, the same strictures do not apply to God who, *by definition,* wholly transcends this spatiotemporal mode. In fact, Derrida's deconstruction of the pretensions of the autonomous, self-identical human subject logically clears the way for an acceptance of the mysterious otherness of the God of Abraham, Isaac, and Jacob. Given the demonstrable fragmentation of our being and identity, our existence in any form, the sense of our precarious personhood slipping out of the grasp of our differential consciousness, cries out for some explanation beyond the trace of *differance* — the very slippage itself.

May one speculate that Derrida's indisposition to praise inhibits his understanding of this crucial matter? In deploying a rigorous logic with the aim of undermining logic, Derrida leaves himself a comic exemplar of the Cretan liar paradox: A Cretan said, "All Cretans are liars." From the beginning of his deconstructive project, Derrida has recognized this quandary. In an early essay he writes: *"There is no sense in doing without the concepts of metaphysics in order to attack metaphysics. We have no language — no syntax and no lexicon — which is alien to this history; we cannot utter a single destructive proposition which has not already slipped into the form, the logic, and the implicit postulations of precisely what it seeks to contest."* [22] As E. Michael Jones has observed, Derridean deconstruction, in attacking the hypostatized "intentionalist self" of the Western humanist tradition, merely succeeds in turning language into a covert absolute.[23] This is the ineluctable implication of the notion that *differance* — the metaphysical offspring of the differential structure of the linguistic sign — "irrevocably surpasses onto-theology or philosophy." [24] Robert Magliola maintains that "Derrida's argumentation is *primarily* a critique of *the way we think about* reality and not a judgment of reality." [25] Hence, Magliola concludes, he is not an "absurdist." But even making such an allowance, there is something factitious in Derrida's *expose* of the metaphoricity of Western philosophy in "White Mythology." "Metaphor is less in the philosophical text ... than the philosophical text is within metaphor." [26]

For the ultimate ontological project, philosophy's highest truth, as Derrida never ceases to argue, is theological; and theology's center has always been approachable only in terms of a kind of metaphor, analogy. Even as God's essence or nature is identical with his act of existing, St. Thomas Aquinas argues, so his knowledge is identical with His act of knowing. Hence man can no more share God's knowledge and reason than he can share God's existence. That is why no individual man can exhaust human nature; there would then be no individual men, since individual beings (except for the Divine Being) are less than their natures: "for if in Peter, man and the act of being a man were not different, it would be impossible to predicate 'man' univocally of Peter and Paul, whose acts of existence are different." Yet this does not mean, St. Thomas continues, that knowledge of God is utterly impossible; that all assertions about Him, based on human metaphorical language, are simply capricious: whatever is "predicated of God and creature" is not merely arbitrary or "equivocal." If there were no real likeness of creature to God, then God's essence would not be the image of the creatures, and He would not know them in knowing Himself." This is as much as to say that God would not be God, and the creatures not His creatures. Likewise, we could gain no inkling of God, could find no "traces" of Him, in nature; and there could be no meaningful distinctions among the arbitrary, equivocal terms that man might apply to God. Therefore, St. Thomas concludes, ". . . it must be said, that the application of the term 'knowledge' to God's knowledge and to ours is neither altogether univocal nor purely equivocal, but according to analogy, which means nothing else but a porportion." [27]

In this passage from **De Veritate**, St. Thomas confronts Derrida's two principal objects: the deconstruction of the autonomous, self-identical human subject; and likewise of absolute, logocentric knowledge of being. St. Thomas specifies the *differance* in human identity; that is, our incompleteness insofar as our existential realization falls short of our essential nature. There is a sense in which what abortionists say about unborn children is true of everyone: we are all only "potentially human." This seems to me simply a more precise formulation of St. Augustine's insight that personal identity is unstable when not supported by grace, an insight most notably realized in his account of Alypius, who found himself unwillingly enthralled by the sight of bloodshed at the gladitorial shows in Carthage. "He was not now the man who had arrived," Augustine writes, "but simply one of the mob to which he had come, a true companion of those who had brought him." [28] This same realization has been noted by a distinguished modern theologian, Hans Urs von Balthasar: "Between that which I actually am or could be or would like or ought to be, and that which I factually live, do, think, judge or experience just now, there gapes an abyss which I can only bridge by virtue of this advance of hope. I never exist completely in my actions and circumstances." [29] One might suggest that Derrida, in proclaiming the abyss within man's personal self-identity, has merely rediscovered sin. Moreover, although he may regard Christianity as the ultimate logocentric ontotheology, it is not the human logos which is placed at the center. "A Christian never has his unity within himself," von Balthasar continues, "nor does he in any way seek it in himself. He does not collect himself around his own center, but rather wholly elsewhere." [30]

By the same token it is no great scandal, not for the Christian at least, that metaphysical discourse is imperfect and oblique — that "the philosophical text is within metaphor." To know Being — absolute necessary Being as opposed to its contingent, created reflections — is to know God. As Aquinas points out, God's very nature entails that it be impossible for man to make univocal predications regarding his Maker, to capture either his essence or existence in human words. Language is the medium of human knowledge, and both are necessarily limited by the intrinsic limitations of human existence. But just because *differance,* the "undecidable trace," haunts our discourse, it cannot therefore be inferred that the same *differance* infiltrates everything about which we speak. That is why our central metaphysical knowledge is neither univocal or equivocal, but analogical: it is incomplete, indirect, if you will, metaphorical. It is not equivocal or, in deconstructionist terms, simply mistaken or meaningless. The very terms "meaningless" and "mistaken," require the concepts of meaning and accuracy even to signify. Likewise, the "signifier" cannot operate without the "signified," even if the latter is always absent and inaccessible. As C. S. Lewis quips, "the **Romance of the Rose** could not, without loss, be rewritten as the **Romance of the Onion.**" [31] Now neither the rose nor the onion *is* (or is the same as) the erotic favor of a beautiful lady, but the former provides the better analogy. If Derrida were completely right, if language were altogether equivocal, if the signified/signifier relationship of the sign were completely collapsed, then there would be no way of distinguishing between romantic roses and onions. Where Derrida is right, of course, is in seeing that the rose is *finally* the lady, the lady is not everything one might have hoped, theology is not faith — much less the beatific vision. In the end, it amounts to saying that Derrida's great discovery is that man is not God.

As Robert Magliola points out, according to Derrida, "Any philosophy of presence can be disproven. The contradictory which unseats the conclusion of a philosophy of presence is also illogical." [32] The law of contradiction can perhaps be contradicted; reason can stumble into its own limits and know that its final certainties are matters of speculation, not evidence. Only faith can sustain the mind above the abyss which opens up before naked human reason, and faith can only be a gift, the work of grace.

It is noteworthy, then, that Derrida and deconstructionists generally are reticent regarding the channels of grace, the sacraments; for the sacraments, especially the Holy Sacrifice of the Mass, are the ultimate affirmation in the face of deconstructive "pure negative reference." In the sacraments of the New Covenant, grace is not merely *signified* or *prefigured,* as in the ceremonies of the Old Covenant; in the New Covenant, grace is contained and conferred: word, material sign (e.g., bread and wine), and grace all converge in the Presence of the Word. And the sacraments are made possible by the Incarnation, Passion, and Death of the Word, the divine Logos.[33] The Eucharist is especially significant in this regard in that the Church teaches that Jesus Christ, true God and true man, is "really and substantially contained under the appearance of the sensible signs." [34] The doctrine of the Real Presence in the Sacrament of the Altar of the New Covenant is thus the fulfillment of the Messianic promise — the deconstructive longing for the *deferred* Presence — of the Old Covenant. In this sense, Derrida is true to his heritage of Judaism, which is par excellence the religion of the Book, the deferral of the Presence of the Word.[35] But he might also be seen as the last scion of the Protestant Reformation, which generally displaced the sacraments with an intense emphasis on *writing* — *sola scriptura.* Derrida would seem to have taken this development as far as it can go: he is a Moses who has broken the Tablets and will not re-ascend the mountain, who offers only more wandering — more *erring* — in the wilderness, with the Promised Land endlessly deferred.

It may seem that I have shown that Derrida has merely reinvented the wheel, and there would certainly be an element of truth in this observation. Yet I am convinced that his work is important, if for no other reason than that he unveils the actual tendency of the secularization of Western philosophy and culture during the past several centuries. In exposing the covert dependency of all "logocentric" metaphysics on the concept of God, he demonstrates the emptiness, indeed the fraudulence, of profane humanisms. He proffers a choice (willingly or not) between the deconstructionist abyss or God, between Derrida or Deity. Perhaps Derrida's role in postmodern intellectual life can best be illustrated by comparing him to a fictional character. In Flannery O'Connor's "A Good Man is Hard to Find," an ordinary Middle American family, driving through rural Georgia, falls into the hands of an escaped murderer, who calls himself the Misfit, and two of his companions. While the two companions are shooting the husband, the wife, and the two children, the Grandmother, a "respectable," and rather shallow, Christian lady, pleads for her life: "Pray! Jesus, you ought not to shoot a lady. I'll give you all the money I've got!" The Misfit is not interested in the offer of money ("Lady, there never was a body that give the undertaker a tip"), but he is obsessed with Jesus:

> "Jesus was the only One that ever raised the dead," the Misfit continued, "and He shouldn't have done it. He thown everything off balance. If He did what He said, then it's nothing for you to do but thow away everything and follow Him, and if He didn't, then it's nothing for you to do but enjoy the few minutes you got left the best way you can — by killing somebody or burning down his house or doing some other meanness to him. No pleasure but meanness," he said and his voice had become almost a snarl.
>
> "Maybe He didn't raise the dead," the old lady mumbled, not knowing what she was saying and feeling so dizzy that she sank down in the ditch with her legs twisted under her.
>
> "I wasn't there so I can't say He didn't," the Misfit said. "I wisht I had of been there," he said, hitting the ground with his fist. "It ain't right I wasn't there because if I had of been there I would of known. Listen lady," he said in a high voice, "if I had of been there I would of known and I wouldn't be like I am now." His voice seemed about to crack and the grandmother's head cleared for an instant. She saw the man's face twisted close to her own as if he were going to cry and she murmured, "Why you're one of my babies. You're one of my children!" She reached out and touched him on the shoulder. The Misfit sprang back as if a snake had bitten him and shot her three times through the chest. Then he put his gun down on the ground and took off his glasses and began to clean them.

The Grandmother, we are told, "Half sat and half lay in a puddle of blood with her legs crossed under like a child's and her face smiling up at the cloudless sky." Do we deconstruct this term "child" in Derridean fashion? Does the suggestion of spiritual immaturity it conveys undermine the sign of new-found innocence acquired in her sudden but telling acknowledgement of her own sinfulness and kinship with the Misfit? Is she the Devil's mother, or does her confession of parentage restore her childhood hopes? Probably all of these meanings and more are available in the text, but the deconstructive effort to deny the uniqueness of imaginative literature is overwhelmed by the mysterious power of this passage to make meanings coalesce rather than fragment and dissipate. *I* cannot give a sufficient exposition of how the *childish* old woman becomes *childlike;* I can only point to the grim alternative to her humiliation and death registered in the exchange that follows between the Misfit and one of his henchmen:

> "She was a talker, wasn't she?" Bobby Lee said, sliding down the ditch with a yodel.
> "She would of been a good woman," the Misfit said, "if it had been somebody there to shoot her every minute of her life."

"Some fun!" Bobby Lee said.

"Shut up, Bobby Lee," the Misfit said. "It's no real pleasure in life." [36]

I shall not claim that the analogy is perfect; they never are. Still, there is a sense in which Derrida can be compared to the Misfit, we Christians to the Grandmother. (Liberal commentators, incidentally, have often preferred the Misfit, seeing in him a socially deprived prophet, in the Grandmother a Bourgeois hypocrite, so that certainly fits.) I believe that we need a few Derridas around, to shoot us every minute of our lives. We need the test to our faith, the reminder that our salvation lies not in the theological equivalent of being a "lady," but rather in faith in Jesus. Perhaps we can no more argue with Derrida than with the Misfit; we surely cannot argue with death. We can, however, hope for the moment of grace, the movement of charity, which seems to be what the Grandmother experiences at her life's close. Finally, we can remember that, as the heirs of Western civilization, we must acknowledge that Derrida, like the Misfit, is "one of our own children." This will help us to remember that in the alienated, deconstructed, angst-ridden post-modern world, "It's no real pleasure in life" — unless you "throw away everything and follow Him." [37]

NOTES

[1] "The Critic as Host," in Harold Bloom *et al,* **Deconstruction and Criticism** (New York: Seabury, 1979), pp. 223, 226.

[2] Although the dates of the original French editions are mentioned in the text, the titles are those of the English translations, which have appeared later: **Speech and Phenomena and Other Essays on Husserl's Theory of Signs,** trans. David B. Allison (Evanston, IL: Northwestern Univ. Press, 1973); **Writing and Difference,** trans. Alan Bass (Chicago: Univ. of Chicago Press, 1978); **Of Grammatology,** trans. Gayatri Chakravorty Spivak (Baltimore: Johns Hopkins Univ. Press, 1976); **Dissemination,** trans. Barbara Johnson (Chicago: Univ. of Chicago Press, 1981); **Margins of Philosophy,** trans. Alan Bass (Chicago: Univ. of Chicago Press, 1982); and **Positions,** trans. Alan Bass (Chicago: Univ. of Chicago Press, 1981). "Structure, Sign, and Play" has been reprinted as the tenth chapter of **Writing and Difference** and, in a translation by Richard Macksey, in **The Structuralist Controversy,** ed. Richard Macksey and Eugenio Donato (Baltimore: Johns Hopkins Univ. Press, 1972), pp. 247-65.

[3] **Course in General Linguistics,** trans. Wade Baskin (1959; rpt. New York: McGraw-Hill, 1966), p. 118.

[4] Cf. Hillis Miller, "The Critic as Host," p. 230: "We have no other language. The language of criticism is subject to exactly the same limitations and blind alleys as the works it reads. The most heroic effort to escape from the prisonhouse of language only builds the walls higher."

[5] **Speech and Phenomena,** p. 65.

[6] **Of Grammatology,** p. 71.

[7] **The World, the Text, and the Critic** (Cambridge: Harvard Univ. Press, 1983), p. 214.

[8] **After the New Criticism** (Chicago: Univ. of Chicago Press, 1980), p. 177. Cf. the nagging questions of Guy Scarpetta and Jean-Louis Houdebine in **Positions** (pp. 56, 60-62, 67-68, 79-81, 88-89) in which the two interviewers, especially the latter, try unsuccessfully to elicit from Derrida an affirmation of Marxist dialectic and its exemption from the deconstructive process.

[9] Jacques Monod, **Chance and Necessity,** trans. Austryn Wainhouse (New York: Knopf, 1971), p. 172: "It is perfectly true that science outrages values . . . it subverts every one of the mythical or philosophical ontogenies upon which the animist tradition, from the Australian aborigines to the dialectical materialists, has made all ethics rest: values, duties, rights, prohibitions." Monod tries to save the situation by resorting to "an ethic of knowledge" which man *"prescribes . . . to himself"* (pp. 176-77, emphasis original). Derrida is not so naive.

[10] **Confessions,** IV.1: "Et quis homo est, quilibet homo, cum sit homo?"

[11] **Ibid.,** IV.10: "Tantum dedisti eis, quia partes sunt rerum, quae non sunt omnes simul, sed decedendo ac succedendo agunt omnes universum, cuius partes sunt. Ecce sic peragitur et sermo noster per signa sonantia. Non enim erit totus sermo, si unum verbum non decedat, cum sonuerit partes suas, ut succedat aliud."

[12] **Ibid.,** XI.7: "Neque enim finitur, quod dicebatur, et dicitur aliud, ut possint dici omnia, sed simul ac sempiterne omnia; alioquin iam tempus et mutatio et non vera aeternitas nec vera immortalitas."

[13] See above n. 5.

[14] **Speech and Phenomena,** pp. 134-35.

[15] **Ibid.,** p. 159.

[16] **Ibid.**

[17] **Ibid.,** p. 53.

[18] **Ibid.,** p. 54.

[19] **Conf.** XI.14: "Duo ergo illa tempora, praeteritum et futurum, quomodo sunt, quando et praeteritum iam non est et futurum nondum est? Praesens autem si semper esset praesens nec in praeteritum transiret, non iam esset tempus, sed aeternitas. Si ergo praesens, ut tempus sit, ideo fit, quia in praeteritum transit, quomodo et hoc esse dicimus, cui causa ut sit illa est, quia non erit, ut scilicet non vere dicamus tempus esse, nisi quia tendit non esse?"

[20] **Speech and Phenomena,** pp. 103, 104.

[21] **Conf.** XI.31: "Longe tu, longe mirabilius longeque secretius. Neque enim sicut nota cantantis notumve cantici audientis expectatione vocum futurarum et memoria praeteritarum variatur affectus sensusque distenditur, ita tibi aliquid accidit incommutabiliter aeterno, hoc est vere aeterno creatori mentium. Sicut ergo nosti *in principio caelum et terram* sine varietate notitiae tuae, ita fecisti *in principio caelum et terram* sine distentione actionis tuae. Qui intelligit, confiteatur tibi, et qui non intelligit, confiteatur tibi."

[22] "Structure, Sign, and Play," **The Structuralist Controversy,** p. 250.

[23] "Metaphysics as Tarbaby: Intention, Deconstruction and Absolutes," *Center Journal,* 1, No. 2 (Spring, 1982), 29.

[24] **Speech and Phenomena**, p. 135.

[25] **Derrida on the Mend** (West Lafayette, IN: Purdue Univ. Press, 1984), p. 18.

[26] **Margins of Philosophy**, p. 258.

[27] **Quaestiones Disputatae**, XI.ii.11: 'Quidquid autem est in Deo, hoc est suum proprium esse; sicut enim essentia in eo est idem quod esse, ita scientia idem est quod scientum esse in eo; unde, cum esse quod est proprium unius rei non possit alteri communicari, impossibile est quod creatura pertingat ad eamdem rationem habendi aliquid quod habet Deus, sicut impossibile est quod idem esse preveniat. Similiter etiam in nobis esset: si enim in Petro non differret homo et hominem esse, impossibile esset quod homo univoce diceretur de Petro et Paulo, quibus est esse diversum; nec tamen potest dici quod omnino aequivoce praedicetur quidquid de Deo et creatura dicitur, quia si non esset aliqua convenientia creaturae ad Deum secundum rem, sua essentia non esset creaturarum similitudo; et ita cognoscendo essentiam suam non cognosceret creaturas. Similiter etiam nec nos ex rebus creatis in cognitionem Dei pervenire possemus; nec nominum quae aptantur, unum magis de eo dicendum esset quam aliud; quia ex aequivocis non differt quodcumque nomen imponatur, ex quo nulla rei convenientia attenditur.

"Unde dicendum est, quod nec omnino univoce, nec pure aequivoce, nomen scientiae de scientiae Dei et nostra praedicatur; sed secundum analogiam, quod nihil est aliud dictu quam secundum proportionem."

[28] **Conf.** VI.8: "et non erat iam ille, qui venerat, sed unus de turba, ad quam venerat, et verus eorum socius, a quibus adductus erat."

[29] **Convergences to the Source of Christian Mystery**, trans. E. A. Nelson (San Francisco: Ignatius Press, 1983), p. 14.

[30] **Ibid.**, p. 129.

[31] C. S. Lewis and E. M. W. Tilyard, **The Personal Heresy** (London: Oxford Univ. Press, 1939), p. 97.

[32] **Derrida on the Mend**, p. 35. See also p. 45.

[33] Henr. Denzinger et Clem Bannwart, S.J., **Enchiridion Symbolorum, Definitionum et Declarationum** (17th ed., Friburgi Brigoviae: Herder, 1928), #695, #849.

[34] **Ibid.**, #874.

[35] For Derrida's interest in the Judaic sources of his own thought see "Edmond Jabes and the Question of the Book" and "Violence and Metaphysics: An Essay on the Thought of Emmanuel Levinas," chapters 3 and 4 of **Writing and Difference.**

[36] **A Good Man Is Hard to Find and Other Stories** (New York: Harcourt Brace Jovanovich, 1955), pp. 28-29.

[37] I wish to thank my North Carolina State colleagues Barbara Baines and Tom Hester for their invaluable comments on the earlier draft of this paper.

Presidential Address

by

Earl A. Weis, S.J.

We have been accustomed to receive quarterly an excellent news-letter, edited by Monsignor George Kelly, but the fact that we receive it regularly and that it arrives in such good form should not blind us to the fact that it is a fine means of communication both within and out-side the Fellowship and that it is doing its job effectively. The issues featuring Father Ronald Lawler's review of Vol. I of Dr. Grisez's **The Way of the Lord Jesus**, Doctor William May's report on the CTSA's continuing seminar on moral theology, Monsignor Kelly's review of Doctor James Hitchcock's book, **The Pope and the Jesuits**, and the two reports of Cardinal Joseph Ratzinger's views (one on post-conciliar Biblical criticism, the other on a variety of topics including the unity of faith, Vatican II, the missionary activity of the Church, and the Holy Spirit) — all these five issues were a real contribution to the discussions going on in the Church.

The board met in September and devoted itself most substantially to a discussion of the program for this meeting. The speakers you have heard were decided on at that meeting as well as, naturally, the topics they would address.

The day after the directors met, the Cardinal Wright Award cere-mony took place in downtown Chicago, with the award being presented to the well-deserving Father John A. Hardon, S.J. Before a record crowd in the audience at the Hotel Continental, Father Hardon reminded us that "no amount of mere scholarship or erudition is enough to defend what we believe. Not today. We must join scholarship with constant prayer for divine light. We must combine erudition with meditation in God's presence on the mysteries of our faith." Once again it is a pleasure to thank John and Eileen Farrell and their committee for the arrange-ments of a beautiful occasion.

The bishops of the United States have come to the Fellowship on at least two occasions for nominations to the Catholic-Anglican Dialogue committee and to the group of consultants for their forth-coming letter on women. In both cases the nominations were accepted.

Other opportunities have been given on other occasions for direct input into their projects.

My special thanks go to the officers — Doctor Joseph Boyle, Doctor Joseph Scottino, and all the members of the Board of Directors, whose fidelity to their duties and sense of responsibility have been such a source of inspiration.

We are also grateful to Mr. Chauncey Stillman, who through Father Richard Roach, S.J., has pledged a sum of money to the Fellowship so that it might bring speakers from abroad.

We are still a young organization, and the question must remain open as to whether or not we can survive in the character with which we were founded. There are many reasons for thinking that we cannot.

What is the character we had (and still have) at our foundation? We are a group of scholars from different scientific and professional areas, engaged in teaching, research, and other learned activities in a context of loyalty to the Church's magisterium, especially as it is embodied in the Church's chief teacher, the Holy Father.

It seemed simple enough when the Fellowship was conceived. At that time, dissent from the teaching of the Holy Father was leaking into the atmosphere. The reaction to **Humanae Vitae** showed that one was dealing not with a Three-Mile Island type of leakage but with a virtual Bhopal, India situation. The casualties were piling up. The "Catholic" public dissenters on the abortion issue of recent vintage are a minor event compared to what happened after **Humanae Vitae.** At that time, there occurred the Charles Curran strike at the Catholic University of America and the dissent of the Washington clergy, which proved to be such a cross to Cardinal O'Boyle. Not far from that point in time was the infamous report on human sexuality from a committee of the Catholic Theological Society of America. In that organization, moderate and loyal theologians were, indeed, marginalized and not allowed to express their views with weight equal to the committee's. The report was published before it was ever submitted to the general membership or even a general meeting.

We all remember the history, yes, but what is to prevent us from being what we want to be, a counter-weight to dissenters? What is to prevent:

- our being categorized, sometimes even by friends, as just another conservative group.

- our being actually absorbed by other groups, whose loyal goals are similar to ours but whose means are diverse.

— our falling down in the matter of scholarship itself and not doing our *best* work in defense of the magisterium.

— our mistaking our proper contribution, cool scholarship, for the emotion-laden contributions of movements and crusades.

— our considering ourselves an American branch, or a cheering section, for the Congregation of the Doctrine of the Faith.

— our descending to the level of personal antipathy and "odium theologicum" in our dealings with those we should be hoping to persuade.

How can we be what we were founded to be? By remembering who we are: *scholars* loyal to the magisterium. By, consequently, entrusting the leadership of our organization to officers, to helmsmen, who will keep it on course. By raising our voice in protest when we recognize that the Fellowship is diverging from our stated means and goals.

In his address to the cardinals, members of the pontifical household, and the curia, the Holy Father on December 21 outlined a certain ideal for the task set before us — because we want to be scholars, yes, but Catholic scholars, showing not only learning but the virtues of followers of Christ. The Holy Father pointed out that the Church after Vatican II, in carrying out its duty of safeguarding the truth, does not achieve this by passing over in some way the dignity and rights of persons. "What can be hoped is that an equally respectful attitude be always assumed by those persons with regard to the Congregation itself [of the Doctrine of the Faith] when they comment, in private or in public, on its work. And the same principle should also apply to every member of the People of God" since we also should want "to safeguard from all dangers *the greatest good* which the Christian possesses; that is *the authenticity and integrity of his faith*" (*L'Osservatore Romano*, January 21, 1985, page 7).